On Jordan's stormy Banks

On Jordan's **stormy** Banks

Lessons from the Book of Deuteronomy

James E. Brenneman

**Herald
Press**

Scottdale, Pennsylvania
Waterloo, Ontario

Library of Congress Cataloging-in-Publication Data
Brenneman, James E., 1954-
  On Jordan's stormy banks : lessons from the book of Deuteronomy /
James E. Brenneman.
      p. cm.
  Includes bibliographical references.
  ISBN 0-8361-9278-8 (pbk. : alk. paper)
  1. Bible. O.T. Deuteronomy—Criticism, interpretation, etc. 2. Bible.
O.T. Deuteronomy—Meditations. I. Title.
  BS1275.52.B74 2004
  222'.1506—dc22
                                                    2004007030

ON JORDAN'S STORMY BANKS
Copyright © 2004 by Herald Press, Scottdale, Pa. 15683
    Published simultaneously in Canada by Herald Press,
    Waterloo, Ont. N2L 6H7. All rights reserved
Library of Congress Catalog Card Number: 2004007030
International Standard Book Number: 0-8361-9278-8
Printed in the United States of America
Cover design by Anne Berry

12 11 10 09 08 07 06 05 04 10 9 8 7 6 5 4 3 2 1

To order or request information, please call
1-800-759-4447 (individuals); 1-800-245-7894 (trade).
Website: www.heraldpress.com

To our son
Quinn Miguel Plank Brenneman

and

to his grandparents
Mary Kathryn and Gaylord Brenneman
Bertha and Irwin Plank
Mary and James Wenger

"*When your children ask you in time to come, 'What is the meaning of the decrees and statutes that the* LORD *our God has commanded you?' then you shall say to your children. . . . 'If we diligently observe this entire commandment before the* LORD *our God . . . we will be in the right.'"*
Deuteronomy 6:20, 25

TABLE OF CONTENTS

FOREWORD

Deuteronomy may not be the most popular book of the Bible, or even of the Old Testament. It may be a book with little action, consisting primarily of speech or even sermon. Few turn to Deuteronomy for in-depth study.

Why then, one might ask, publish a study guide for this ancient writing. Brenneman provides one answer in the opening paragraphs—Deuteronomy, he suggests, "holds many of the levers for understanding the entire biblical corpus." The message and content of Deuteronomy influenced both the substance and layout of the rest of the Old Testament. The life and teachings of Jesus Christ as told in the New Testament cannot be fully appreciated without recognizing how much Jesus lived out of this tradition. Deuteronomy thus serves as a key for unlocking much of the rest of Scripture.

This would already be sufficient reason for a study guide on Deuteronomy. But that is only a secondary reason. More importantly, Deuteronomy itself points in the direction of life. It invites people to use their "God-given absolute freedom of choice" to choose life rather than death.

As Brenneman repeatedly asserts, "Deuteronomy is a crossroads book." At the boundary of the Promised Land, on the banks of the Jordan, Moses exhorts Israel to look backward. And forward. The look backward reminds the people of their past, their time of slavery and oppression in Egypt, and God's amazing intervention in delivering them from Pharaoh. God was their savior. Through this saving action Israel came to know and understand their God.

The look forward considers life in the Promised Land, after Israel has crossed the Jordan. It raises the vexing question: How will Israeli people respond to this new situation, when Israel no longer needs manna from God, but can grow her own food? Remembering the past is important, but only if it influences how one lives in the present and the future. Israel is at a crossroads. How the people respond will determine whether life in the Promised Land is characterized by blessing or by curse, by life or death.

Such a reality is not unique to Israel, however. All of us, as individuals, as groups, as churches encounter crossroads on the journey, times when we are faced with critical decisions about how to live and respond. It may be at the point of leaving high school or college, when adulthood beckons. It may be a congregation facing declining fortunes in a rural environment. It may the move to retirement. It may be. . . . There are many crossroads which present themselves. The question at each one of them is, "Will we choose life?"

Deuteronomy not only repeatedly presents this question, but also paints pictures of what it means to choose life by expounding upon the law. Of course, this is where Deuteronomy becomes problematic for so many of us, steeped in a contemporary understanding of law, and absolutely persuaded that many of the requirements of Deuteronomy are archaic and no longer normative for us. We may appreciate the wonderful generalities of the Ten Commandments. Or the lofty requirement of the *Shema* so powerfully confirmed by Jesus—"The LORD our God is one LORD; and you shall love the LORD your God with all your heart, and with all your soul, and with all your might." But what about the law prohibiting the eating of pork? Or the encouragement to parents to have their stubborn son stoned? How can these lead to life?

Brenneman's study guide is not a commentary. It does not go into detail on each verse and regulation, but it does provide a wonderful window into Deuteronomy, and how it can and does address those critical crossroads of life.

—*Gerald Gerbrandt, President,*
Canadian Mennonite University

These "studies in Deuteronomy" are meant to invite you, whether alone or in a group, *to study* God's word as diligently as those to whom the apostle Paul and Silas visited in the town of Beroea. It was said of them, "they welcomed the message very eagerly and examined the scriptures every day to see whether these things were true" (Acts. 17:11b). To that end, each chapter has a corresponding series of questions for readers (found in the back of the book, "For Further Reflection") to dive deeper and stay longer in the waters of Deuteronomy before attempting to crossover to that never quite attainable "promised land" of truth.

This book is not meant to be a commentary-study of the book of Deuteronomy. I have provided a short bibliography "for further reading" at the end of this book should any reader wish to pursue in more detail what is offered here for study. The books and commentaries listed there are assumed here, though any variation of interpretation from them is my own. All translations of the biblical text throughout are either from the *New Revised Standard Version* or my own. Throughout, I have also chosen to use the title LORD (small capitals) for the original Hebrew tetragrammaton of the divine name of God.

We will dip into strategic texts within Deuteronomy, sometimes more deeply, sometimes less, but always with the intent to provide for the reader an overall appreciation and understanding of the book of Deuteronomy.

The origins of this book began as Bible studies on the

book of Deuteronomy that I was asked to give at the Mennonite Church General assembly in Orlando, Florida, in 1997. At that time, Herald Press invited me to consider publishing those public Bible studies in the form of a book. As a full-time pastor at Pasadena Mennonite Church and a part-time faculty member of the Episcopal Theological School at Claremont (Calif.), I never found the time to further develop those earlier forays into book form.

In the summer of 2002, I was granted a four month sabbatical from my congregation and, with the generous support of a Lily Endowment Clergy Renewal grant, was able to spend three months as a scholar-in-residence at the Tantur Ecumenical Institute in Jerusalem, Israel. Those three months provided the opportunity to complete this book. Since then, I have had the privilege of teaching an adult education class for my congregation using the material from this book. I wish to thank all those who participated in this class and along the way, who offered advice, asked probing questions, provided new insights, and assisted me in the final version, here presented.

I especially want to thank Father Michael McGary and Sister Maria Nora Onnis of Tantur who provided great support while I was in Jerusalem. My time away from home could not have been possible without the unfailing support of my wife of twenty-six years, Terri Plank Brenneman, and the tacit understanding of our son, Quinn, who was only five years old at the time and who may not truly have understood that his dad was to be gone for three whole months.

Thank you to the folks at Herald Press for their editorial help and encouragement in turning this manuscript into a book.

I dedicate this book to our son Quinn Miguel Plank Brenneman and to his three sets of grandparents, Mary Kathryn and Gaylord Brenneman, Bertha and Irwin Plank, and Mary and Jim Wenger. In the faithful recounting and living of their lives and in their telling of stories from their pasts, Quinn's grandparents transcribe in him a hope in God.

That hope-filled legacy will be his guide as he now stands on Jordan's stormy banks, his whole future before him, ready to possess God's destiny for him.

CHAPTER ONE

On Jordan's Stormy Banks

> On Jordan's stormy banks I stand
> And cast a wishful eye
> To Canaan's fair and happy land
> Where my possessions lie.
> — Samuel Stennett, 1787

Why study the book of Deuteronomy? Second only to the book of Leviticus, Deuteronomy is perhaps the last book in Scripture that most Bible readers might select for in-depth study. The instinctive reluctance to study the book of Deuteronomy is not altogether unwarranted, but, as this book hopes to show, such misgivings about the book of Deuteronomy must be overcome, if we hope to understand the rest of Scripture. Like the wizard in the famous children's tale, *The Wizard of Oz*, the book of Deuteronomy holds many of the levers for understanding the entire biblical corpus. More precisely, the wizards or editors or compilers of the Older Testament have as one of their controlling editorial levers, the message and content of the book of Deuteronomy. Like the lion, the scarecrow, and the tin man in the *Wizard of Oz*, the stories of the characters throughout the Older Testament, including the stories of judges, priests, kings, and prophets, seem to be guided almost unseen by the wizardry of the book of Deuteronomy. A Deuteronomy-like perspective, itself, influenced even the layout of the Old Testament canon.

More significantly, for Christian readers, the life and teachings of Jesus in the New Testament can hardly be appreciated without some understanding of the book of Deuteronomy. Clearly, one of the scrolls most cherished by Jesus and the gospel writers, especially Luke, was the scroll of Deuteronomy.

Still, the reluctance of most readers of Scripture to open their Bibles to the book of Deuteronomy seems justified. On the one hand, and upon first glance, there seems to be no reason for the book of Deuteronomy in Scripture. In reading the story of the great escape of Hebrew slaves from Egypt and their dizzy wandering around the desert of Sinai, one can literally eye-jump from the end of the book of Numbers to the end of the book of Deuteronomy and not miss a beat in the story. The book of Numbers concludes with the wandering band of ex-slaves gathered at the banks of Jordan River waiting for the grand entrance into the "Promised Land." That's exactly where they still are at the end of the book of Deuteronomy, still on the Jordan's eastern banks. In other words, one could remove the book of Deuteronomy from Scripture and not miss a thing in the narrative flow as presented to the reader.

Deuteronomy is basically all words and no action. In fact, the Hebrew name for the book, *Devarim*, as with other books in the Torah, comes from the first words of the book (1:1): "These are the *words* that Moses spoke . . ." For the activist reader, the self-admitted nature of the book as one of mere words and no action, seems to recommend skipping the book altogether. But for the wizard behind the book's structure, the opening lines of the book provides one convenient way for structuring the whole book (1:1; 4:44, 6:1, 12:1, 29:1). The tally of words in Deuteronomy includes three sermons by Moses (chaps. 1–4; 5–11; 29–32) and, for good measure, a law scroll thrown in between (chaps. 12–28).

Deuteronomy's Structure

The structure of Deuteronomy roughly coincides to some old treaties discovered in the archives of a Hittite capital which date fourteen to fifteen centuries before Christ. These Hittite treaties describe political arrangements nearly a whole century before the events described in the book of Deuteronomy are said to have taken place. These old treaties, sometimes called suzerain-vassal treaties, illustrate covenants made between an imperial overlord and his subject rulers. In the case of Deuteronomy, the suzerain would naturally be God and the people of emergent Israel would be God's subjects. The treaties were drawn up using six principal elements: 1) the preamble stating the primary signers of the treaty; 2) a short history told from a particular point of view, usually that of the overlord; 3) stipulations or obligations placed on the underling as evidence of his loyalty to the overlord; 4) rules for public readings or covenant signing and renewal ceremonies, alongside defined places for depositing the treaties; 5) a list of divine witnesses to the treaty or in some cases mountains, clouds, winds, and other phenomena thought to be divine; and 6) blessings and curses which spell out the sanctions for obeying or disobeying the covenant. In Scripture we have glimpses of some covenant-making ceremonies and some of the other above elements as well as the kind of events that might provoke the making of such treaties (Gen. 15:7-19; Exod. 20 and 24:3-8; Josh. 24; 1 Kings 20:1-35; and Jer. 34:8-22). Clearly, Israel was aware of and participated in the world of embassies and alliances, treaty-making events, blessing and cursing formulations, and other forms of what we might refer to in our own time as international diplomacy. The chart below illustrates not only the overall structure of the book of Deuteronomy, but also how close many of the international treaty features pre-dating Israel's own covenant structure coincide with the book of Deuteronomy as well.

Structure of the Book of Deuteronomy

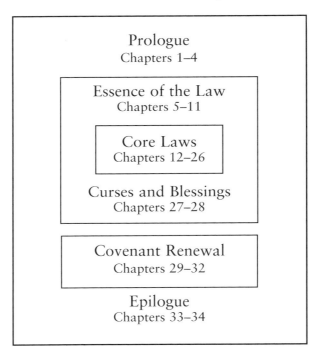

Treaty Covenant Structure in Deuteronomy (based on Hitite/Assyrian treaties)

4:44–49	Preamble
5–11	Historical Background (ten "Words"(5); plus commentary (6-11)
12–26	Conditions and Stipulations
27; 31:10–13	Publication (Covenant Ceremony and Public Reading)
30:19	Divine Witnesses
27–28	Blessings and Curses

A Historic Find

The law scroll (Deut. 12-28), inserted as it is between sermons two and three of Moses, looks a lot like it could have been similar to, or the same, law-code found much later in Israel's history quite by accident. In the story recounted in 2 Kings 22, the child prince, Josiah, and his courtiers decide to renovate the temple. Like so many ancient artifacts found in modern renovations in Israel today, the contractors unearthed an old scroll vault, called a *geniza*, where used scrolls were deposited according to Jewish law. One of the old scrolls found in the rubble sent spiritual shock waves throughout Josiah's court.

There's a tale going around about a monk who accidentally ran across an old manuscript in the archives of his Abbey. In shock, he was heard exclaiming, the text says, "celebrate," not "celibate." The young king Josiah seemed to undergo similar shock in reading the words of the ancient manuscript he discovered in his temple renovations. Upon reading it, Josiah immediately began a huge reformation, not unlike the one Protestants recount in the history of the church. The kinds of reforms enacted by Josiah (2 Kings 23) look like they had as their blueprint the laws outlined in the central law-code we now read in the book of Deuteronomy. That Josiah was shocked at all and that he immediately instituted practices found in the scroll suggests that whatever the scroll described was not known in Josiah's day, if ever.

Guided as it appears he was by the words of a newly discovered book of Deuteronomy, Josiah went about destroying all idols and worship centers of other gods. Like the book of Deuteronomy, he demands that all worship be centered in Jerusalem under the one and only God. He even removed heretofore "legitimate" sanctuaries to the LORD that were located throughout the land since ancient times. The Passover festival, which had not been celebrated since the days of the judges, some 300 years earlier, was reinstated as prescribed by the covenant scroll he found. The storyteller concludes this Reformation account with nothing but praise for Josiah (2 Kings 23:24-25): "He established the words of the law that were written in the book . . . found in the house of the LORD. Before him there was no king like him . . . nor did any arise like him afterwards." But then, to make explicit the link between the book found by Josiah and the book we now call "Deuteronomy," the writer borrows the very language of Deuteronomy's most famous commandment (Deut. 6:5) to further praise Josiah, who, "turned to the LORD with all his heart, with all his soul, and with all his might." And he did so, "according to all the law of Moses" (2 Kings 23:24b-25).

Even though it was found much later in Israel's history as suggested above, the book of Deuteronomy (certainly its law section) now added an important element in the telling of Israel's early history that may have gone unnoticed, and certainly had gone unheeded, prior to its discovery in Josiah's remodeling project. In the final form of Deuteronomy, this law scroll apparently found its way into the treaty-form that was well known at that time. Whether or not, as some scholars have argued, the book of Deuteronomy was composed in Josiah's time (or even later) and inserted back into the Torah story to give Josiah's reforms Mosaic authority need not concern us here. Whatever the history of the origin of the book of Deuteronomy, we now know the book in its awkward literary placement in Scripture and must try to understand it accordingly.

As a book of words and no action, the perceptive reader will soon notice that the book of Deuteronomy seems quite redundant in parts. Not only does Moses repeat the old stories of the Exodus, but the book of laws in Deuteronomy repeat large portions of the earlier Book of the Covenant found in Exodus 21–23. If we were led to ask earlier, what does it mean that here is a book of words said to be spoken by Moses to a people not going anywhere—at least, not yet? Now, further questions are provoked: What does it mean that in the book of Deuteronomy Moses repeats many of the stories and many of the laws already given in the biblical books preceding it? Why all the repetition? Doesn't such redundancy simply accentuate doubts about why the book of Deuteronomy is even necessary? On the one hand, then, there seems to be little reason for the book of Deuteronomy in Scripture.

Deuteronomy at the Crossroads

On the other hand, there is every reason the book of Deuteronomy is in Scripture. As much of the rest of this study of Deuteronomy will attest, the *fact* of its redundancy, the *fact* that the book of Deuteronomy seems bent on repeating some earlier stories and laws, but not others, may be just the clue to the very reason *for* the book of Deuteronomy in Scripture. In fact, from its opening lines, Deuteronomy hardly finds this form of repetition an embarrassment. Knowing that an observant reader or listener would notice these changes between God's first revelation in Exodus and that of Moses' update in Deuteronomy, the book opens with an explanation of sorts. Already in verse 5 of the first chapter, the narrator tells the inquisitive reader or listener that the job of Moses, here, is to "expand" or "explain" or "interpret" the law (Torah).

It is no small admission in the opening lines of the book of Deuteronomy that the narrator tells us that the words to follow are those of *Moses*! In the Exodus narrative, the same laws were there expressed as having come directly from God in divine speech or, in the case of the Ten Commandments written twice by God on stone tablets without the assistance of Moses. In fact, the other four books of the Pentateuch (Torah) are all told, as it were, by an omniscient narrator.

Not so the book of Deuteronomy. Moses is explicitly said to be the primary narrator. The book is meant to be a book of reminiscences, one step removed from the kind of direct divine revelation as heard in the first four books. Moses simply recounts the earlier events. He becomes the oral and literary link back and up to God and forth and down-line to a new generation. The bridge between "back then" and "now" is no longer that of direct-speech from God to Moses, but now the book unfolds through the "mere" words of Moses as the opening lines assert (1:1): "these are the words *of Moses*." In these opening words of the book of Deuteronomy, an incarnational "bottoms-up" doctrine of Scripture is suggested. God's direct word becomes increasingly circumscribed as Scripture unrolls into accounts of Israel's future from here on out. So much so, that by the time the third section of the Hebrew Bible, called the Writings, is compiled, three of the books (Esther, Song of Solomon, and Ruth) do not even have the word God in them. The largest book in the Writings, indeed in the Bible, the book of Psalms, has God speaking only nine or ten times (Ps. 2, 50, 81, 87, 89, 95, 105, 110, and 132) out of some 600 times the first person singular "I" is used in the Psalms. Increasingly, for all future generations after Moses, the mediated nature of revelation as human speech becomes the dominate medium of revelation in Scripture. Even the prophetic divine speeches, indeed, whenever God speaks in Scripture, it is important to remember that these are usually, if not always, "*reports of* divine speech." In Scripture, divinely-inspired, fallible, human words are seen as capable of infallibly linking us to God, even claiming to speak for God. Deuteronomy is the first explicit admission of this all-pervasive reality in Scripture. Deuteronomy lies at the crossroads of divine-human revelation.

Apparently, for the compilers of Scripture, a second accounting of the law was deemed important. At least, a second copy was called for, even an updated version, a new revised standard version. The very name Deuteronomy, the Greek (and then, Latinized) title of the book, derives from its purpose to restate the law, a "second" (Greek: *deutero*) "law" (Greek: *nomos*). The expression, itself, derives from the laws of kingship in Deuteronomy (17:18) that require the king upon ascending the throne to have a "copy of the law" (lit. a "second law," a *deutero-nomos*) made and read at regular intervals. In fact, this need to amplify, revise, and clarify the old laws of Exodus suggests that the book of Deuteronomy, already when inserted here, was no doubt understood to be a replacement for the earlier versions. As we will see, the importance of Deuteronomy, a second version of the law (Torah), lies in its updating function.

Precisely because of its redundancy, its repetitions, its updating function, some scholars have argued that the book of Deuteronomy is one of, if not *the*, most important book in the Old Testament. Others have called it the first "New Testament" in the Old Testament, the "theological center of the Old Testament." What seems clear is that in its final placement within the Torah, the book of Deuteronomy holds, perhaps, the most prestigious place in all of Scripture. It serves as a theological capstone of the Torah (the first five books of Scripture) and a literary bridge foreshadowing the travails and blessings of Israel from the Promised Land to exile (Joshua to 2 Kings). To understand the book of Deuteronomy is to better understand all that precedes and follows it in Scripture.

The book of Deuteronomy is a crossroads book, between memory and remembrance, between grandparents and grandchildren, between promise and fulfillment, between there-and-then, here-and-now, and yet-to-come, between old and new. It is no small thing that the words of Moses ring out in perpetual song between Jordan's stormy banks. As these studies in Deuteronomy hope to show, in some sense, all of us still stand on the eastern banks of Jordan casting a "wishful eye to that fair and happy land." As it must be.

CHAPTER TWO

Between Then and Now

Memory believes before knowing remembers.
—*William Faulkner,* Light in August

Read Deuteronomy 1–4

In his tenth novel, Light in August, William Faulkner recounts the earliest memories of five-year-old Joe Christmas, a mulatto child abandoned at birth on Christmas day on the doorsteps of an orphanage in Faulkner's mythic Yoknapatawpha County in Northern Mississippi. Christmas intuits and stores in his little mind the understated actions, the inferred comments, the inexplicable subtleties of others all around him, never knowing, as no five-year-old could, the racism he would only know by experience and come to understand in hindsight years later. In a sense, Christmas believes in the memories instilled by others long before he is capable of remembering for himself what those memories only foreshadowed. Life is like that for most of us. Memories are stored inside us much like seeds from a variety pack just waiting to blossom in ways and kinds not fully known to us in their planting. Long before we even know it, we are acting out or reacting to the stories and experiences of others around us, whether recounted to us explicitly or lived out in front of us in shadowy, passive testimony.

"Life must be lived forward," reasoned Søren Kierkegaard, the melancholy Danish philosopher, "but it can only be understood backwards." The book of Deuteronomy asserts that life must be lived forward, but it challenges its listeners never to forget the past, either. It is a book of memory and destiny. Deuteronomy's main character, Moses, remembers on behalf of the next generation, what they themselves have not yet experienced, but will, as will all of us who hear his telling.

The three sermons of Moses in the book of Deuteronomy (Deut. 1–4; 5–11; 29–32) come off sounding a bit like the ramblings of an old man. Indeed, they are. One-hundred-and-twenty-year-old Moses, redundant and insolent, sets out to retell the same-old, same-old stories heard around the campfires of wandering nomads for at least forty years. Especially in chapters 1–4, Moses rehearses his memory of when God rescued the Hebrew slaves from Egypt and served up manna and quail in the wilderness. Moses bends the ear of his people one last time. In fact, some have suggested the book of Deuteronomy is the "last will and testament" of Moses just before he disappears into the wilderness to die in an unmarked grave. Surprisingly, "no one knows his burial place to this day" (Deut. 34:6). What an ignoble end for such an illustrious career. Sad, really. Moses is reduced to sermonizing one last time lest the new generation forgets him and, more importantly, forgets its own history.

Moses' sermonizing reminds me a little bit of my wife's ninety-year-old grandpa who self-published a little book just before he died entitled, *The Bible Means What It Says!* In it he waxes on about such topics as the evils of playing baseball on Sundays, watching too much TV and, FORNI-CATION (always spelled in capital letters). May grandpa rest in peace. God knows he didn't appear to want us to. Moses was a bit like grandpa, or that older person we all know who tells a younger crowd what it was like to go through the Great Depression or what dodging the draft in the crazy 60s was like, or why we call music played on CDs, "albums," or what we mean by the phrase "carbon copy." When it comes to describing Moses' role to his audience, the rock group, Meatloaf, has it just about right in their song,

"Objects in the Rear View Mirror." "If life is just a high-way," they sing, "then the soul is just a car / and objects in the rearview mirror / may appear closer than they are." Moses acts as a rearview mirror to his young congregation to remind them that the lessons of the past are not as far away as they may, at first, appear. He's lived long enough to know that history does repeat itself, maybe especially so, if no one ever looks back. But Moses isn't simply an old geezer in a sports car looking in the rearview mirror, his goal is to send his children of faith safely into the sunset, hair flying in the wind, radio blaring to Meatloaf's insightful lyrics.

Like any decent older person, Moses may have worried about the new generation of "baggy-panted, ear-ringed retro-cool" or their equivalent born in the refugee camps of Sinai and other "tag-a-longs" who had not themselves experienced the Exodus first hand. A little calculation of generations might help to explain the situation. Say, a person who was twenty years old at the time of his or her escape from Egypt had a child right about that time. By the time the escaped slaves reached their first real stop at Kadesh-Barnea, an oasis in the Sinai, that newborn would also be twenty years old with, perhaps, another child on the way. Again, by the time they wandered around some twenty years more before Moses begins his "re-education seminar in the desert," as Bruce Feiler describes the book of Deuteronomy, most everyone listening to Moses by this time would be twenty years old or younger. Indeed, we're told by Moses at the beginning of his first sermon that the only two persons still living from the days of the Exodus experience, were Joshua and Caleb (1:35-40), and, of course, Moses. So now, before he dies, Moses sets out to interpret the divine Torah to the grandchildren of those first escaped slaves, a whole new generation. This is all that remains for Moses to do before he disappears forever from the scene, to pass on the spiritual DNA to those who were born in between the great Exodus event and the yet-to-come experience of entering the Promised Land.

Notice how Moses recounts the "good ole days." In the first three chapters of Deuteronomy alone, the expression "at that time" is repeated seven times (1:9, 18; 2:34; 3:18, 21, 23) to introduce the retelling of portions of the now old story. Moses also reminds his own generation, the so-called geriatric crowd, that they, including him, will not enter the Promised Land for a host of reasons (1:35; 2:14), not least of which is their age. They simply won't be around when that day comes.

From the point of view of the older folks, those of Moses' generation and, perhaps, even one generation later, Deuteronomy is a catechism of sorts with Moses presented over and over as the model teacher (1:5; 4:1, 14; 5:31; 31:19, 22). Like a master teacher passing on faith memories and old, now revised laws, from one generation to the next, Moses does his job well. From the point of view of the book of Deuteronomy, the meaning of the old stories and old laws would now partly come from theological reflection on those laws and stories, not simply a verbatim replay of divine direct-speech as in the "olden" days. In one among several telling examples, Moses instructs parents that when they are asked by their children to explain the meaning of the law, as children inevitably do, they should follow Moses' example, as it were, and explain or interpret the meaning for them (Deut. 6:20). The very meaning of the word, "Torah," means "instruction." And Moses models in Deuteronomy how one goes about instructing the new generation in the ways of Torah.

Called to Remember

The first three chapters of Deuteronomy are mostly told about events that happened "at that time . . ." somewhere in the past (1:9, 18; 2:34; 3:4, 8, 12, 18, 21, 23). A lot is at stake here. Memories can be forgotten, the loss of which can prove fatal to our true identities. Emergent Israel was no exception. Forgetting their past, good and bad, would've also been fatal to emergent Israel's identity. So, lest these desert pilgrims forget to look in the rearview mirror every now and again, even as they lurched forward into the future, Moses reminds them repeatedly, "do not forget!" Like a mantra this phrase resounds throughout the rest of the book of Deuteronomy (4:9, 23, 31; 8:11, 14, 19; 9:7; 25:19). For three chapters then, Moses is describing events that happened "at that time . . ." back there, back then, past tense, as if to say, "Don't ever forget!"

But, then abruptly the first verse of chapter 4 opens with an emphatic, "So NOW: today, here, present tense.

> "So now, Israel, give heed to the statutes and ordinances that I am teaching you to observe, so that you may live to enter and occupy the land that the LORD, the God of your ancestors, is giving you."

As if to say, "So now, today, give heed to what I say and pass it on." Moses also instructs the people to "Make them known to your children and your children's children" (4:9, 10; 6:2, 7; 11:19) so as to never forget. Moses includes this new generation into his confession with a liturgy (5:2-3): "The LORD our God made a covenant *with us* at Horeb (Deuteronomy's name for Mt. Sinai). Not with our ancestors did the LORD make this covenant, but *with us, who are all here alive today.*"

The shift from "at that time . . ." language to "so now" language shifts the meaning of Deuteronomy from the "there and then" to the "here and now" of the next generation and to every generation thereafter that read these words. "So now," Deuteronomy becomes a catechism for each one of us reading it today. Moses incorporates all subsequent generations into the Torah story. By means of a liturgical confession, the "here and now" of the text is not meant for its hearers to simply read about these wandering believers, but to *become* them, to enter their story. In a similar sense, for Christians, the shared cup and bread of the Lord's table becomes the means by which all who share in this ritual feast *become* one with those first disciples gathered around Jesus. We do this "in remembrance," but not of some old dusty past, rather of a living experience of that past "here and now." So too is Moses' retelling of the past. It is not meant to be some remote account for its own sake, but an invitation to become a part of the narrative of this people, today.

Like any good novel or piece of literature, the author(s) want very much for the readers, whenever they happen to pick up their tale, to enter fully into it, to join with the characters in their failures, their joys, their lives. The literary nature of Deuteronomy is no different. Its chief protagonist, Moses, wishes for all, including us, who hear his story about the failures of older Israel to experience them as if they are our own. But also, and more importantly, Moses calls his congregation to remember God's mercy toward older Israel as being God's mercy toward all who hear his words.

The main lesson that emerges from this initial probe into the early chapters of Deuteronomy is simple enough: "God calls us to remember." And not only to remember what it was like "at that time," but also to pass on those memories to a new generation. Our identity as people, as people of God, hinges on God's call through Moses to remember and to pass on those memories. Memory, though a bit choppy and not altogether foolproof, still links us to a remembered past that helps us define ourselves as people of destiny. Memory constructs identity. If you don't think so, ask yourself: Which is more important for lasting meaning in life, our actual experiences, fleeting as they are in time and space, or the memories that remain when the experience is over? Would you trade a good mind for remembering life's experiences in return for twenty additional years of otherwise healthy living with no memory at all? What is the meaning of former United States President Ronald Reagan's presidency to him, if, due to the ravages of Alzheimer's, he can no longer remember having been president at all?

Experience also tells us that sometimes it is important to distance ourselves from the past, even to forget, in order to go on at all. An inability to forget can lead us to hold on bitterly to desires for vengeance and to negative, hurtful experiences that poison our will to live. Sometimes we must, as Isaiah reminds us, "forget the former things," or as the apostle Paul reiterates, "lay aside the weight that so easily besets us." Sometimes, we must forget. But, equally important are some things, good and bad, that we must never forget. It may be that we must forgive, even if we never forget. But to simply forget may invite a repeat of old buried memories, having forgotten their cruelty to us, and in turn, foist them anew, if unconsciously, on others. Such forgetfulness does no one, least of all us, any lasting good. So Moses says (4:32), "Ask now about the former ages, long before your own, ever since the day that God created human beings on the earth; ask from one end of heaven to the other." We must ask of times past, hone our memories, then restate, rethink, renew, retell and, perhaps, forgive the past over and over until its truths canyon deep into our gray matter, deep in our pre-conscious and unconscious selves, deep into our souls— never to leave us even if fate robs us of our conscious memory. Our souls need the mirror of memory.

The Bible, like the book of Deuteronomy, is preoccupied with this memory core. The word for remembering (Hebrew: *zahkar*) appears 169 times in the Older Testament. Memory in the Bible, however, is not a rigid, sclerotic memory. It is fluid. Deuteronomy models this memory-making flexibility. For example, Moses doesn't create water tight accounts of the past. Like ancient singers of tales long before him, Moses shapes his reminiscing for a new generation. His is the kind of remembering that grandmas and grandpas do who highlight their past, who gather in pieces and bits their remembrances, in order to tell their grandchildren about who they are and who they might become. Moses rehearses a second version of the Exodus story and the Law traditions, all the while updating it. He asks the new generation to retell it in their own way to the next generation after them (8: 14-18): "Do not then forget the LORD your God who brought you out of the land of Egypt, out of the house of slavery; who guided you through this vast and dreadful wilderness. . . . Remember the LORD your God; it was the LORD who gave you this strength."

How do we remember our pasts? How do we live out those remembered pasts? Deuteronomy, the first new testament of the Old Testament invites us to do our first works over, to revise, to at least reexamine everything, to go back where we started "at that time," or as far back as we can, to travel our road again. Deuteronomy invites us, as the poet James Baldwin suggests in our remembering, "to sing or shout or testify or keep it to ourselves, but to know from whence we have come."

Deuteronomy, the second version of a remembered past and a second look at the Law, also suggests that when we pass on "at that time" traditions to the "so also now" settings of our lives, we must also allow some adjustment to the new realities, to new readers, to a new generation.

Living Here and Now

Do we in our own churches today try to rigidly mimic the New Testament church? In doing so, we may be deceiving ourselves that such an imitation is, strictly speaking, even possible. But more importantly, we may have misread God's call to remember a static call, only "there and then" living. The spirit of Deuteronomy is more creative than that. Christ was a good reader of Deuteronomy. When Jesus said "you have heard that it was said," he was patterning his speech after Moses when Moses said "at that time." When Jesus said, "but I say unto you," he might as well have been borrowing from Moses' emphatic, "so now!" God calls for a spirit-driven memory with a creative edge. Pass it on, but do so in accordance with the present context.

What is God calling the church to be in the twenty-first century? To be the church in the twenty-first century! God is not calling the church of the twenty-first century to become a rigid mock-up of the first century church. For sure, we must safeguard that memory, but we must not memorialize it in stone. In good deuteronomic fashion as expressed by the apostle Paul, God still wants to write the law on our hearts, not on tablets of stone.

As Scripture readers, we may need to update our exegesis, our readings of certain texts, our interpretations. Deuteronomy, as a book, remembers past traditions, an earlier covenant, an old testament, but then has Moses revise it for a new readership. If biblical authority is taken seriously, then the model of passing on the faith that Deuteronomy shows us should become for us as canonically authoritative as the very content of what is being passed on. Deuteronomy encourages us, even requires us, to creatively tell the same-old, same-old story in a new way. Deuteronomy shows a people standing at the crossroads of life, how to remember and pass it on.

Telling the Stories

How do we remember our pasts? As a member of a historic peace church, I trace my spiritual roots to the sixteenth-century Anabaptist movement. One cannot recount the stories from that time without noting the terrible persecution and martyrdom born by these early radical reformers. Rehearsing the stories of martyrdom is not meant to carry on age-old animosities, nor to remain in a victim mindset, nor to preserve a particular ethnic grouping. Rather, stories from the past are told so as to make claim to the long line of tagalongs to God's salvation history. Our stories are commingled with the stories of others rescued by God from utter extinction. In faith, as it was for those in the desert of Sinai who never actually experienced the Exodus for themselves, the Torah story becomes our own. We are called to remember "our" exodus story, "our" *Deutero-nomos* (law-retold), our *Deutero-muthos* (story-retold) as an act of faithfulness.

In my family, ever since childhood, the story of "the massacre" of 1757 is forever etched in our memories. My great-grandparents eight generations back helped to settle Pennsylvania. The new government of Pennsylvania generally had good relations with the indigenous Delaware tribes as late as 1757 until, that is, Fort North Kill was built without regard for their territory.

As the story is told, the youngsters gathered to pare apples in the front room of the house when the dog stirred. When Junior opened the door to see what was up, he got shot in the leg. There were plenty of guns and ammunition in the house and the boys were sharpshooters. However, the father refused to let them use the guns for protection. The whole family fled to the basement praying for refuge there. A fire was set, and as the house burned, the family tried to escape out the basement window. All but three were killed and scalped. Father and two sons were held captive by the Delaware for eleven years when Father escaped. Eventually, after some treaty signings, the two sons were released. Both sons later often returned to the tribe to fish, trap, and visit. They had become reconciled to their mortal enemies.

Our parents told us the story as instruction in the faith. We learned early on that there were principals of a nonviolent faith greater than survival. It became explicit in the telling that had our young cousins started shooting "at that time," the whole family might have perished. I would not be telling this story today. The lesson stuck in the telling and retelling. It's as if God were telling us, "Remember, you too were once captives and I brought you out and redeemed you." Our family had known the exodus. The Torah story retold. The memories we access, the stories we retell, shape not just our ethics telling us how we should live, but these memories told also shape our relationships telling us who we are and who we will become.

In her book, *Family Puzzles*, award-winning *Boston Globe* columnist, Linda Weltner, describes how our version of a memory, how our version of "at that time" events still impact our relationships even now. She tells of playing with her granddaughter, Jess, and how it brought back a flood of memories of what it was like playing with her own daughter, the baby's mother, Laura. One day, she exclaimed to her daughter Laura, "I'm having as much fun with Jess as I had with you when you were that age." Laura replied rather certainly, "that's not so, Mom." She went on to rehearse years of her mother lamenting about how hard it was to raise kids. Linda, the author, was emotionally stung by her daughter's memory. For the first time she realized that she had created a particular version of herself. What her daughter had said was true. As the mother of Laura, she had always emphasized the hardship of being the wife, following grudgingly behind her husband's every career move. She had complained a lot, and felt the burden of childcare alone. This hard memory became the catalyst for a more profound healing in Linda's life. She contemplated keeping her own version of her remembered past, but asked herself, "at what cost?" She found herself at the crossroads of remembering two versions of her story. She had always chosen to travel in only one direction in the retelling. So she sat down and went back over twenty-five years and gathered together another string of memories about her life that she had long ago buried. She rewrote her story of mothering Laura, which in part now reads: "I recall . . . the thrill of holding a beautiful, but sticky infant in my arms immediately after delivery; watching her slip peacefully into sleep while breastfeeding; the rush of joy when Laura stretched up her pudgy little arms to be lifted." Mother Linda was able to remember a different past than the one she had always accepted and retold before. She was able to rewrite, retell, refocus her memories to include much good without overlooking the bad. She too had a second telling, a *deutero-nomos* story.

One of our great tasks in life is to challenge each other to recall positive stories, stories of inspiration and faith. What memories can we tell of overcoming adversity? What memories can be shared that recall ethical intent and moral guidance? What memories do we have of God's salvation in time of need? Recall, update, and pass them on. In the words of the model before us (11:18-21), Moses tells us to put these memories in our heart and soul, to bind them upon our arms and foreheads, to write them on our doorposts, to tell of them before sleeping and upon rising.

Younger generations of readers are reminded of their need for some older folks around to tell the way things used to be "at that time." In my own congregation of some baby boomers and mostly younger adults, our faith has been kept alive, certainly renewed, by ninety-year-old Dorothy Smoker. In her heyday with us she was a straight-shooting, honest-to-God, honest-to-us type person, a former missionary who got converted by those she went to serve. We could not get enough of her wit, her stories, her spiritual failures, and her amazing victories. She brought the East Africa revival to our doorstep and passed it on to us. She is our spiritual grandmother, our spiritual lifeline to a God of mighty grace, a God whose arms are outstretched to gather us beneath her wings like a mother hen. In our congregation, we are who we are, in part, because Dorothy keeps the old, old story alive for us. Bless her and all those who help us cross over to the past. Our spiritual identities depend on just such living memories.

To all the memory keepers of our lives, ravaged though you may be by the frailty of age, we say, "Bless you!" Like Moses, you bridge for a new generation that distance between who we once were and who we may still become.

To those reading these texts who are older, more Moses than Mickey, do not fear making your way through years of memories. Share all you can with the younger crowd. But also remember, it is they, not you who in all likelihood will cross over the Jordan far into the new millennium and beyond. Follow the example of Moses: go ahead and preach three long sermons, but like Moses, refrain from expecting the youngsters to follow lockstep behind you. You too may need to offer up a *deutero-nomos*, a second version, a new last will and testament that allows a new generation to hear and receive the old traditions in new and living ways. More than anything else, the younger generation longs for the blessing of its spiritual forebears as they take the old, old stories and make them their own.

So now, today, to all of us, with pasts good or not, whether old or young, it doesn't much matter. Moses invites us into the Torah (Christ) story. Thanks to God and our fore-parents in faith and history, we who were at one time no one in particular, have now been made one people. We now have a past, a tale to tell. We now have a remembered past that is every bit ours as it was Moses' and his people or Christ's and his disciples. Our call is to remember the good news, and if need be, change it a bit, and then, by all means, pass it on.

CHAPTER THREE

Between Grace and Law

The law of the Lord is perfect,
reviving the soul.
—Psalms 19:7

Read Deuteronomy 5

Apparently, in Massachusetts you can't eat peanuts in church. In Gary, Indiana, you can't attend a theater less than four hours after eating garlic. There's a law still on the books in Sault Sainte Marie, Michigan, against spitting upwind. Carrying a lunch bucket on the street in Riverside, California, is against the law. In Oregon, it's illegal for a dead juror to serve on a jury. Imagine that! In Los Angeles, you can't use the U.S. mail service to complain about cockroaches in your hotel room. And in Hollywood, it's still illegal to drive more than two thousand sheep down Hollywood Boulevard at one time. These and other seemingly silly laws are recounted by Barbara Seuling in her book appropriately titled, *You Can't Eat Peanuts in Church and Other Little-Known Laws.*

From the ridiculous to the sublime, from ancient times to now, we have lived and sometimes died by the rules and regulations foisted on us or chosen by us to guide our lives. Jesus' observation concerning the poor might be extended to say that commandments and laws, like the poor, will "always be with us." Do's and don'ts, "thou-shalts" and "shalt-nots" are a fact of life no matter how much we chafe or complain or rebel against them. We need laws. We need commandments, if for no other reason, than to keep all those lawyers busy helping us find the loopholes. In the same vein of ambivalence toward the law, the American financial tycoon, J. Pierpont Morgan, was said to have once remarked: "I don't want a lawyer to tell me what I can't do; I hire him to tell me how to do what I want to do."

The ambivalence toward laws in general has often transmuted into outright contempt for the laws of Scripture. W. C. Fields admitted that he spent a lot of time looking through the Bible for loopholes. He isn't the only one. So many of us picture the God of Scripture as a cranky old school teacher who seems to be always chiding, coercing, nagging "his" students into grudging compliance with ever growing lists of inane or downright dumb laws. So many of us who read the laws of Scripture feel like Dennis the Menace standing in the corner again, wondering if God simply created all these laws to take the fun out of a kid's life. Lacking a sense of irony, we can spend a lifetime and millions of dollars trying to skirt the law, but are among the first to use it to our advantage when we've been wronged or mistreated. Something is out of kilter here, especially with regard to a biblical understanding of the law.

Could the Psalmist really have meant it when he wrote, "The law of the LORD is perfect, reviving the soul" (19:7)? Is it possible to have such high regard for the statutes, laws, and testimonies of God in Scripture that we experience them as the Psalmist did, as perfect instruments reviving our flagging souls? The book of Deuteronomy helps focus our response to these questions by recovering the spirit of the commandments, especially the spirit of the ancient biblical law code popularly called The Ten Commandments.

In the United States, much debate has gone into whether the posting of the Ten Commandments in schools, courthouses, and other government buildings infringes on the "separation of powers" clause in the U.S. Constitution. This is not the place to argue the pros and cons of such a contentious issue. However, even if we were to post the Ten Commandments in public places, which version would we post? Within the Bible itself there are three separate accounts, the first being listed in Exodus 20. This set of commandments was shattered by Moses in a fit of pique which forced God to reissue a second version in Exodus 34. Then there's Deuteronomy 5, a third form of the command-ments. Even then, one could argue that the version in Exodus 20 lists not ten commandments, but arguably fourteen, which Christians and Jews reduce to ten . . . but, which ten? Exodus 34 has seventeen do's and don'ts whereas Deuteronomy 5 has fourteen, again reduced to the famous ten by both Jewish and Christian readers. In their liturgies, most Protestants and Jews favor the commandments in Exodus 20, whereas Roman Catholics tend to favor the commandments listed in Deuteronomy 5. Among Roman Catholics, Anglicans and Lutherans, the first commandment begins with the command: "You shall not make for yourself an idol. . . ." Among the Orthodox and Reformed Christian communions, the first commandment begins a verse earlier with: "You shall have no other gods before me." Moreover, for Catholics, the dictate against adultery is the sixth com-mandment; for Jews and most Protestants it's the seventh. Some sensitive Catholic catechisms thoughtfully exclude the wife from the list of farm animals which one might covet by making the coveting of a neighbor's wife a separate com-mandment.

So the ordering of the commandments alone would pose a distinct set of problems for any public posting of the Ten Commandments without favoring this or that particular religious tradition. But that is only the tip of a much more problematic iceberg when it comes to fully appreciating the meaning and intent of these commandments. Unfortunately, all Christian traditions have done a disservice to the spirit of these laws. All Christian traditions, when ordering their top ten commandments among the various options already noted, lop off from their list *the* most important part of the entire set of commands that follow. In the Jewish tradition, the first commandment includes the all important statement which says: "I am the LORD your God, who brought you out of the land of Egypt, out of the house of slavery; you shall have no other gods before me." The Christian traditions merely see the description of God's having saved the people from slavery in Egypt as prologue to the Ten Commandments, *not* an *essential* part of their various lists. For Jewish interpreters, by contrast, not only is the first command embedded in an explicit account of God's salvation history, but the other nine commandments are also to be understood as a response to this saving gospel embedded in the first commandment.

The Law and the Gospel

The old canard that the Jewish interpretations of Scripture are mostly legalistic renderings of the law in contrast to more "enlightened" Christian readings are shown in this instance to be just plain wrong. It is the Christian rendering and ordering of the Ten Commandments that have severed the gospel from the law, in part, due to their bias about Old Testament Law as generally understood. The Law (Hebrew, *torah*) of Jewish tradition has always included within it the gospel message that God has saved Israel at God's own initiative and by God's grace. Torah, for Jews, contains within it grace and law, story (Hebrew, *hagadah*) and ethics (Hebrew, *halakah*), gospel and commandment. If Jewish interpreters have, at times, emphasized one side of Torah to the exclusion of the other, they are no different than Christians who have done the same in emphasizing only the grace, gospel, and story parts of the New Testament to the exclusion of the law, ethics, and commandments found there. Christians avoid speaking about what the apostle Paul called the "law of Christ" and some even go so far as to exclude the relevance of the Sermon on the Mount, which by all accounts is portrayed by Matthew as a new Sinai event, to some far off millennial event. All this to avoid the sometimes even harder sayings of Jesus. Jesus, portrayed as the "new Moses" on the mountain, was sometimes even more exacting than certain laws of the Older Testament. Mark Twain, the great American novelist, remarked, "It's not the laws of the Bible I don't understand that are the hardest for me, it's the ones I do understand." So, many, if not most, Christians edit out of their experience or understanding those very New Testament laws they most clearly understand but are hardest to follow. They do this because of a basic misunderstanding of the Torah-Christ story and their readiness to believe, contrary to the evidence, that the Old Testament is without much grace and the New Testament is devoid of legal material.

It is important for any reading of the Ten Commandments, indeed, in reading any legal tradition in the whole of the Older Testament, to remember that every law code of the Hebrew Bible, especially its crown jewel, the Ten Commandments, lies embedded within the larger story of God's mighty deliverance of emergent Israel by an undeserved act of grace. As just one excellent example of the spirit of the law within the Older Testament, nearly six out of every ten laws in the book of Deuteronomy have as the motivation for why they should be obeyed, a very compelling reason: "Remember that you were a slave in Egypt and the LORD your God redeemed you from there" (24:18). Obedience embedded in grace.

When the Rabbis are asked, "If the Ten Commandments are so important, why weren't they placed at the very beginning of the Torah?" The Rabbis reply with a story: "A king came into a city. He asked his people, 'May I rule over you?' They replied, 'Have you done us any good that you should rule over us?' The king then built a wall for them, brought them water, and fought their battles. Then, he asked, 'May I rule over you?' And they replied, 'Yes, indeed.'"

You see, it's no accident that the Ten Commandments find their place in Scripture only after God saved an enslaved people from mighty Pharaoh, from drowning in the Red Sea, from starving in the desert, and from being slaughtered by the Amalakites. It is precisely and only *after* Moses recounts the mighty acts and deeds of mercy by God (Deut. 1–4), that he then reminds them of the Ten Commandments that God gave them, as well (Deut. 5). In a sense, the list of commandments, though utterly important, would always be embedded in God's unmerited favor and saving grace.

Which Laws Still Apply?

Jewish tradition, early church renderings, Christian readings, and scholarly opinion have always recognized priorities of importance within the law traditions of Scripture. Certainly, the Ten Commandments have been almost universally understood as analogical to more modern notions of constitutional law under which the many case laws of Scripture are subsumed. Thus, the many laws of Deuteronomy (as in Exodus) begin with the Decalogue and branch out from there. Such prioritizing of the law is a fact made clear by the structure of books which contain them. David Noel Freedman, in his book, *The Nine Commandments*, shows how even a larger corpus of the Older Testament, called by him "the Primary History" and the first history of the world (Genesis–2 Kings), finds itself structured in relationship to the "Ten" Commandments. For Freedman, each biblical book in this Primary History is linked to one of the commandments. As to why he speaks only of nine commandments in the title of his book, the reader will have to consult Freedman herself. I don't want to spoil the mystery of his approach. But, Jesus also seems to prioritize the law in the Torah and Prophets even more exactly. In his response to a question posed to him by a precocious lawyer who asked him which was the greatest commandment in Scripture (Matt. 22:34-40), Jesus, as it were, sifts through the whole of the law in Scripture, and summarizes that the laws in both the Torah and the Prophets can be fulfilled by just two Old Testament laws. The first is found in Deuteronomy 6:5, "You shall love the Lord your God with all your heart, with all your soul and all your might."

And the second is found in, of all books, Leviticus: "You shall love your neighbor as yourself" (19:7). So, prioritizing our legal obligations seems to be a requirement of a discerning mind.

As we've seen, some laws stay on the books long after they have any meaning for us at all. If no one still eats peanuts in church in Massachusetts or drives cattle down Hollywood Boulevard or if no one much cares if they do, then these laws die a natural death either by attrition or change of circumstance. No legislature has the time or the obligation to go back and clean up all these old case laws that have run their course. The same is true of the laws of Scripture which have run their course. For example, no Christians that I know of and only some Jews would insist on following the law in Leviticus 19:19 that admonishes a person not to put on a garment that is made of two different materials. For most of us living in a world of polyester and cotton blends, such a law makes little sense. For most of us, even its original meaning has become obscured and lost over the course of time. As we'll argue later, this should pose no great problem for many, since all of us have lived our lives between old laws and new ones.

What *does* matter for Israel, and should matter to us, whatever rules and regulations God outlined there and then, or here and now, whether eventually ridiculous or eternally divine, all our laws should remain within the context of God's saving acts on our behalf. Our first response to obeying the laws of God, whether those dictated in ten relatively clear-cut commandments or others negotiated by us as believing communities over time, must be accepted as response to God's loving, saving initiative. We shouldn't need any more incentive to obey than that, though we often still do.

Beyond being motivated by the gospel underlying every law, such rules and regulations (do's and don'ts) are also simply part of what is good and holy in the created order. In the words of the Psalmist, "the law of the LORD is perfect, reviving the soul" (19:7). Or as the apostle Paul says in Romans 7:12, "the law is holy, and the commandment is holy and just and good." To speak of God's grace as a replacement to God's law is neither biblical nor possible. As has been shown, the very structure of the Ten Commandments and the other biblical laws link grace and law together. We admit as much whenever we insist that something is the "gospel truth"! To a single mother with kids, the law requiring a deadbeat dad to support his children sounds an awful lot like grace. To an inner city family, outlawing semi-automatic guns may sound a lot like grace. Property laws may have a ring of pure grace to the widowed victim of an unscrupulous landlord. The gospel truth is that there is no world where two or more people relate to each other or to God that will not also require rules to live by—period. Even in a world where grace abounds and where the just live by faith, there will be a need for grace-filled boundary setting and lawgiving.

Apostle Paul was frustrated with the Old Testament law mostly in the sense that so many Jews couldn't translate the gospel part of their Torah (law) about God saving them from Egypt into the New Testament setting. If Paul tended to devalue the law part of the Torah in favor of the gospel portion, he did so, in part, for strategic reasons. If he could just get the Jews to focus on the story portion of their law, they might more easily see that the same God who had crouched down into huts and hovels with slaves in Egypt and led them across the Red Sea to freedom was the same God who crouched down into a cradle in Bethlehem as a renewed attempt to save people from the sins of violating good and holy laws. Paul thought Jews who read Torah concentrating on God's mighty acts would clearly see that "Christ is the climax of Torah" (Rom. 10:4).

But Paul also thought the world was about to end. He didn't have time to announce a new set of laws to live by, a new set of appropriate boundaries by which relationships could flourish in the newly formed Christian communities. What is clear from a chronological understanding of Paul's letters to the emerging church is that as time went on, his epistles became increasingly filled with the practical "how to's" and "do's and don'ts" so necessary for healthy living. So too, did the New Testament gospels, which were written still later, contain within them a new set of "thou-shalts and shalt-nots" for this new generation of believers. As was noted above, and restated here, if the Jews of Jesus' day were tempted to sever the new gospel from their old laws, the Christians in days since are equally guilty of trying to sever the gospel from the good news and holiness of the law.

Some recent self-help books have suggested that the highest form of psychological development and authenticity lies in the autonomous individual's evolution to living in a world without law. Such sentiment is fine at the level of theory, but the Bible is much more practical than that. The Bible offers no such utopian picture of the autonomous self where love and law are enemies. In the Bible, the truly authentic person is the one who relates to another person (human or divine), in love to be sure. But, that love is measured by real life responsibilities and duties. Paul's greatest soliloquy on "love" found in 1 Corinthians 13, is full of practical rules and measures defining that love: don't be rude, be patient, be kind, don't insist on your own way, and so on.

The paradise of the Bible is not a place where there will be no laws. The goal and dream the Bible has for a good and just society is not a place where laws are suspended, where there are no longer any laws regulating how we relate to each other or to God. Rather, paradise is a place where we will obey the laws established by God and those negotiated by us because we want to for the good of everyone. What makes heaven heaven is not paradise without laws, though it may be a place without need of lawyers. Rather, heaven will be a place where we have internalized the laws that we all know to be "holy and just and good," a place where we'll understand more completely the gospel of law, a place where the law becomes a grace for reviving our souls.

Ethics vs. Action

If the law, as understood by Scripture, is a haven of holiness, then holiness can no longer be defined by splitting our doing from our being. Richard Foster, in his book *Streams of Living Water*, defines holiness as "the ability to *do* what needs to be done when it needs to be done" (82-86). Here he stands in a long line of those who associate the law with simply that which "we do." He then suggests, in keeping with good Holiness tradition within which he stands and with much of modern psychology, that such actions are of "secondary significance" to the essence of holiness. "Of primary significance," he says, "is something far deeper, far more profound. Of primary importance is our vital union with God." "Action," he concludes, "follows essence." This is Foster's endorsement of the cherished mantra of modern times, often articulated best by the German philosopher Heidegger, that "being precedes doing."

Allow me to be a bit subversive of this popular thesis. Notwithstanding the orthodoxy of the Holiness tradition or the popular myth of "being over doing," can it truly be argued that action follows essence, that "being" is more fundamental, more authentically human or Christian to holiness than "doing"? Is it true that somehow essence or authentic being is the main ingredient of holiness? Is it the case that actions are merely the effect of being holy? Any student of history will recognize in these distinctions the old dichotomies between law and gospel, Protestant orthodoxy over Roman Catholic orthopraxy, "old" testaments and "new" testaments, Jewish legal traditions, and Christian grace traditions.

The great Jewish philosopher, Emmanuel Levinas, in his book *Ethics and Infinity*, corrects these false distinctions, whether articulated by Protestants, Holiness tradition, or modern psychology's quest for authentic wholeness. Levinas argues, though not in these exact words, for an even deeper understanding of holiness. He suggests that since essence (or being) is always and forever "being-in-relationship with another," then ethics (the science of "doing") and ontology (the science of "being") are *essentially* (using the language of either Foster or Heidegger or others) co-terminus. We can never truly speak of existence before ethics, being before doing, essence before action. In fact, we must speak of ethics and action in the instant of existence because existence is always existence-in-relationship and existence-in-relationship always involves ethics or law!

Existence-in-Relationship
Commandments 1-2

If the Ten Commandments in Deuteronomy 5:6-21 (or in Exod. 20) are about anything, they are about existence-in-relationship. The first four commandments emphasize our relationship with God, the remaining commandments speak to how we are to live best in relationship to one another. The first two commandments especially circumscribe our relationship to the one, if not the only, God. Evidence within the Bible and outside it suggests that these first two commandments were given precisely because people then, as now, have always been tempted to devote our lives to a myriad aims, things, ideas, beliefs, and transcendent projections as our ultimate realities. We create gods and idols of our own, though we seldom call them that anymore. We imbue our ultimate commitments with sacred meaning, though we may not call it that, either. Still, whether it is a particular belief system, a particular sacred book, a particular nation-state, or a particular ideology, we do or are tempted to invest in these particularities god-like devotion. These first two commandments address the human tendency to polytheize and to replace a relationship with the living God with all lesser gods or human projections.

Commandment 3

The third commandment confronts us with the very personal, even the most personal, relational aspect of identity, our names, and more specifically, God's name. Whether or not you've ever had your mouth washed out with soap for swearing or using God's name "in vain," this commandment recognizes the adolescent tendency within us all to bring dishonor to God by invoking God's name falsely or carelessly. I can remember the insulting names we used to call our despised ninth grade geometry teacher, Mrs. Bullard. Now, Mrs. Bullard wasn't God, though sometimes she seemed to think she was, standing in the halls between classes watching for the slightest infraction for which she swooped down with her disciplining scowl and lecture. Behind her back, we called her Mrs. Bull-Turd, Mrs. Buzzard, Mrs. Bull-Dog, and other less complimentary names. Though, in her case, she did live up to her name at times, still it was a sign of a deeply broken relationship between her and her students evidenced in our dishonor and disrespectful naming.

The judicial act of placing one's hand on the Bible and "swearing to tell the truth, the whole truth and nothing but the truth, so help me God," carries over the ancient covenant treaty formulas which invoked God (or the gods) as witness(es) to our end of the bargain in upholding our covenanted relationships. In a sense, we are employing an internal check of divine retribution, just like the ancients did before us, to help guarantee our veracity. But, sadly to say, as the recent impeachment for perjury of a sitting President of the United States suggests, such incentives nowadays meet with only limited success. Lying under oath in God's name has become all too common. In Jewish tradition the fear of insulting God in this way, of even potentially using God's name in inappropriate ways, led to the still used custom among some Jewish communities of never uttering the personal name of God, ever. Whatever else this commandment cautioned against, it was a warning about using God's name to impugn God's character, whether that is cursing, lying, or associating it with matters of questionable moral character or simply using the name of God inappropriately in *any* context. One can hardly have a relationship with anyone at any time, if one doesn't, at a minimum, honor that most important identity marker linked to their person, their name. Certainly, a relationship with God is no exception.

Commandment 4

Being in relationship with God entails joining the rhythm of life as God established it in creation. If psychologists are correct in asserting that one of the most basic and earliest developmental stages in human formation involves trust, then the fourth commandment addresses this primal relational category. The Sabbath commandment invites us to trust God, to trust life, to trust the rhythm of nature. In the first version of this commandment in Exodus 20:8-11, the rationale for this trust comes in the form of God's having rested on the seventh day of creation from all God's work. In ancient times, the gods were a fretful bunch who demanded of their human subjects a 24/7 work week, every day, all year long. By contrast, this commandment was "good news" (gospel) to the over-employed, exhausted masses. Initially, at least, Sabbath-keeping was about God *keeping* God's children sane, healthy, relaxed, refreshed, alive, more than it ever was about God's children keeping the Sabbath. Given the hectic, busy lives of just about everyone I know nowadays, this law sounds more like grace than not.

If trust in the rhythm of God's creation or if sheer human exhaustion aren't good enough motivations for keeping the Sabbath, Moses updates the Sabbath commandment in Deuteronomy (5:12-15). It's important to see that Moses adds the short phrase at the end of the first line, "so that your male and female slave should rest the same as you." Then instead of appealing to the creation story as the key to their motivation for keeping the Sabbath as did the Exodus version, Moses gives the standard motivational rationale that he uses throughout the rest of the book of Deuteronomy for keeping any and every law. Keep the Sabbath, Moses says, *because* "you were once slaves in the land of Egypt and the LORD God brought you out . . . therefore, the LORD God commanded you to keep the Sabbath day." Not only does

Moses make the Sabbath commandment a necessary blessing to Israel, he turns the Sabbath law, like so many of the other expansions of law within Deuteronomy, into one of social justice legislation for current slaves who need a day off. Of course, this is just the role the Sabbath rest commandment will later play in the social legislation of the Jubilee laws (Lev. 25) and Jesus' own ministry of Jubilee. In those expansions, even the land deserves a long Sabbath rest. The question really comes down to this, do we trust God enough, whether in our daily work load or even in matters of working hard for social justice, for us to take a Sabbath from work, politicking, labors, and human effort, trusting that God will return on the next workday to help us and others out of bondage into freedom?

Commandments 5-9

The next five commandments in descending order from the more serious offense to the least serious clearly underscore that healthy existence is existence-in-relationship. Honoring our parents, not murdering, not committing adultery, not stealing and not lying, all enhance the quality of our communal life under God. One youngster once pointed out to me that the word "adultery" has another word inside it: "adult." She didn't know just how perceptive she truly was. All these commandments, not just the one about adultery, are earmarked for adults. They challenge grown-ups not to break the rules of being a good adult. God calls us to grow up in our faith and grow up in our faithfulness.

In our society we use the word adult in odd ways. We take a store where X-rated videos and magazines are sold and we call it an adult store. We have Web sites where people are shown breaking the sixth or seventh commandment (depending on who's counting) in multiple ways, and we say those are adult sites. Of course, these are adult stores or sites, but not in the sense that we end up modeling for our children that what they are witnessing is mature behavior or the way grown-ups should relate to each other. Indeed, all these

commandments are meant to teach adults not to break the
rules of being an adult, the cardinal one being, though not
mentioned, serving as role models to our children.

I'm sure what the perceptive girl didn't realize in her
exegesis of the word "adultery," was that even the commandment about honoring our parents was, initially, not
meant for children her age. She may find relief in that fact.
To be sure, parents have often used this commandment,
along with the ones about stealing and lying, to challenge
their children to be more obedient. In itself, such challenge is
not wrong. However, the commandment about honoring
parents, when seen in its Ancient Near-Eastern milieu, invites
adults to honor their adult parents. What better example to
the next generation coming along behind those of us who are
of parenting age, than to love and cherish and care for our
adult parents into their old age. The best way to raise children,
I was once told, is for moms and dads to love each other.
This is quite true and I would also add, to love and honor
their adult parents. Certainly, when it comes to stealing or
lying, what better opportunity do we as adult learners have
to teach the younger generation the truths of these commandments than to obey them ourselves?

The commandment about murder deserves a word or two
more. I have used the more restrictive word "murder"
instead of "killing" as an attempt to distinguish between the
two Hebrew words that describe this heinous act. The
Hebrew word used in this commandment (*ratsach*) can be
contrasted with the more general Hebrew word for killing
(*harag*). In the various law-codes in the Bible, the same word
used in the commandment describes a whole range of homicide from intentional to unintentional murder. In modern
parlance, we describe these various levels of homicide by
degrees: first degree, second degree, and third degree murder
or pre-meditated or involuntary homicide. Like now, so also
then, depending on the degree of intention, the severity of
penalty was meted out. For the person who accidentally
killed another (Deut. 4:42), the penalty is always less severe,

even to the point of providing for such a person the chance to flee to six "sanctuary cities" (Josh. 24:4-6) in refuge from revenge killing. The death penalty, often by stoning, was reserved for more premeditated acts of murder. Of course, even here there were exceptions, the three most prominent being Cain's intentional murder of his brother Abel (Gen. 4), the premeditated killing of the Egyptian by Moses (Exod. 2), and David's cruel murderous plot against Uriah the Hitite to cover up his adulterous affair with Uriah's wife, the beautiful Bathsheba (2 Sam. 11–12). Cain, against all expectation, has the gall to plead for mercy from God for having killed his brother. Amazingly, God grants Cain mercy and merely bans him from the premises. Moses, too, ends up running into the desert when he's confronted for his murderous act. David— though having committed both adultery and murder, both acts for which the death penalty was warranted, to say nothing of his lying, coveting, and stealing—gets off rather leniently. He does suffer the loss to death of his son from this illicit liaison. Still, his legacy and dynasty remains secure. Such mercy is especially telling when Saul's whole family, except his one invalid grandson, gets annihilated for Saul's sins, though not for the sin of first degree murder.

The commandment against murder does cover all degrees of homicide, but not necessarily killing, say in self-defense or warfare or a state-sanctioned death penalty. Certainly, as we have seen, mercy isn't automatically revoked from one who breaks even this commandment. With respect to these other forms of killing (war, self-defense, etc.), it is altogether reasonable to draw inferences from this commandment in a developing response to killing of all types. Later understand-ings—especially the example of Jesus, or later arguments of what constitutes a "just war," or again in questions of what is "cruel and unusual punishment," or still again in instances of indiscriminate killing of nuclear weapons—might be seen as reasonable expansions of the commandment, though not inherent in the language itself. Such expansions, as was argued for in chapter 2, are part of the interpretative process necessary in clarifying the meaning of this or that commandment in new contexts, but a reader should be explicitly aware of extending a text's meaning in this way.

Commandment 10

The final commandment prohibits coveting, that is, the desire to possess that which belongs to another. In the patriarchy of the time, this included a man's wife, alongside all his other possessions. In light of the above discussion about drawing out further meanings from a text bound to its own historical context several observations are in order.

Readers today would have little problem suggesting that the limited view of a wife as property must be abandoned, whereas it is still proper to infer from this last commandment that one must not covet another's wife. Given our more egalitarian context, an even more expansive inference can be drawn to include a prohibition against coveting another's husband as well. Such necessary inferences and expansive readings of texts are reasonable, though not inevitable. In a similar way, it is reasonable, as was suggested above, to extend the meaning of the murder command ("you shall not kill") to other instances of taking the life of another, as well. As will be developed below, the connection between covetous desire and murder is direct, making the commandment not to murder and the commandment not to covet inextricably linked.

As commentators have long been aware, the final commandment which prohibits covetousness is altogether different than the other nine. In each of the other cases, specific *actions* are prohibited or required, whereas, this commandment has to do with *motivation*. The commandment as written in Exodus (20:17) uses the Hebrew word translated as "covet" (*tachmod*) twice, whereas the version in Deuteronomy (5:18) uses two Hebrew words, "covet" (*tachmod*) and "desire" (*tittaveh*). The words are nearly synonymous, though not quite, even in English. The book of Deuteronomy is quite adept at trying to articulate motives either for keeping the commandments, as we have seen, or, in this case, underscoring motivations behind disobedience as well. What better way to do this than to verbally link covetousness with desire.

In the many works of René Girard he has shown repeatedly that the root causes of violence in all its forms is "mimetic desire," or what might be called the desire of acquisition. That is, though innocent enough to begin with, our natural inclinations to imitate others, to become like them, soon turn into the desire to acquire what another person is and has. In time, this basic drive to imitate becomes a felt need to possess and before long, if left unchecked, it leads to murderous intent to get what another has by any means at our disposal. No wonder the final commandment, which in a sense, encompasses all the other commandments, especially those having to do with people-to-people relationships, warns the faithful away from the age-old primal urge to covet what belongs to another. Such covetousness, as the stories of Cain and David so graphically illustrate, inevitably leads to the breaking of most, if not all, the other commandments. It was Cain's jealous desire to be Abel, to mimic Abel's acceptable sacrifice, that led him to ultimately murder his own brother in order to possess his blessing. David's desire of another man's wife led him into adultery, murder, lying, stealing, dishonoring his own family, and breaking covenant with God. In every case it is just such acquisitive desire that serves as the *motivation* for the *actions* to which the other nine commandments warn against. Certainly, Jesus when he addressed the question of ethics in his Sermon on the Mount understood the motivations behind one's actions as key to understanding all other commandments, whether five, ten, or one hundred. And so, Jesus centered his "but I say unto you" supplements to the old laws on the desires of the heart. In this respect, he merely extended the tenth commandment's concern about attitude to those matters of law that he addressed in his sermon.

The Ten Commandments distilled by Moses have been understood by many generations since as the moral foundation of our own legal traditions. Even today their influence is apparent as a quick survey of the Internet suggests. Type the words "the Ten Commandments" into your web browser and it turns up many versions of these historic laws. You'll find "The Ten Commandments of" or "for" Gun-Haters, Dog Owners, Love, Good Historical Writing, Personal Computer Ownership, Leadership, Wealth, E-Commerce, Parenting, Power-positioning, Making It on Your Own, Travel, Tattoo Care, and much, much more. Most of these, of course, are flippant borrowers of the form, missing altogether the substance of the Ten Commandments. And most of them, like so many later Christian understandings, miss the spirit of the commandments altogether, as expressed in the balance between gospel and law inherent in the Jewish understanding of these great laws. In their navel-gazing, egoistic understanding of themselves, these often silly updates of the Ten Commandments miss almost entirely the utter relational thrust of the originals. The originals focused the Law to promote existence-in-relationship, not simply expressions of self-generated autonomy. The originals, like the Torah itself, are deeply relational, in this sense, perfect and holy and good, capable of reviving the soul.

The Ten Commandments are about being in relationship, about being and doing simultaneously, about grace as law or law as grace, and about chosen obedience. That obedience is co-terminus with what it means to be authentically human, wholly human, holy people. The commandments are laws mostly for adults, mature people who no longer pretend that serving a higher law means serving no law at all. That's fantasy. Nor are people truly whole or holy who take pride in rebelling against right and just laws. That's naiveté. From the biblical perspective, people who are whole and complete never rise above the law as if to leave obedience to those of lesser developed faith. Rather, the truly whole person is the one who has learned to love the law, who sees its value for regulating human interaction, who does not need a lawyer or cop or judge threatening punishment in exchange for obedience.

The authentic person follows the law from a deeper sense of obligation and duty to others and in response to the benevolence of God.

God gave us ten relatively straightforward commandments to live by: don't worship false gods, don't limit God to homemade images, don't misuse God's name, rest one day a week, honor your parents, don't murder, don't commit adultery, don't steal, don't lie, and don't covet. Pretty basic. Perhaps, everything we need to know, we did learn in kindergarten or Sunday school or on our parents' knees, or down by the riverside on a Sabbath afternoon, waiting.

CHAPTER FOUR

Between Silence and God

*Imagine a man [or a woman] in whom the tumult of
the flesh goes silent, in whom the images of earth, of
water, or air and of the skies cease to resound. His [or
her] soul turns quiet and, self-reflecting no longer, it
transcends itself. . . . Think of them falling silent,
turning to listen to the One Who created them. . . .
Think of this encounter, seizing, absorbing, drawing
the witness into the depths of joy. Eternal life would
be of a kind with this moment of understanding.*

—St. Augustine, Confessions

Read Deuteronomy 6–11

"Between sea and sand" might be the ancient equivalent
of our quip "between a rock and a hard place." "Between
sea and sand" expresses the predicament of the wilderness
wanderers in the book of Deuteronomy. To their backs were
the waters of captivity. The primordial myths throughout the
region all told of great sea monsters who sought to devour
all who ventured in the ancient seas, whether the Great Sea
(today's Mediterranean) or Lake Timnah or the Bitter Lakes
or the Sea of Reeds, all lying between the Nile River and the
Sinai desert. The miraculous crossing of the Sea of Reeds on
dry ground by the people of the Exodus and the drowning of
the Egyptian army, would later be associated by Isaiah (51:9-10;
cf. Ps. 89:10) with the original creation when God divided

the sea in two, creating dry land. Egypt, itself, would later receive the nickname Rahab (Ps. 87:4) which was the name of the great sea monster of primordial chaos as an apt description of emergent Israel's deepest fears. So, on the one hand, Moses was leading a people who to go back would be certain death by drowning.

On the other hand, facing them was the Sinai desert, often referred to as "24,000 square miles of nothing," nothing, that is, except sand and formidable mountains. In a place where the average rainfall is only about an inch and a half a year, water is your first and last desire. Go wandering in the desert for a day, forty days, or forty years, and water becomes your life. Food ranks a close second. And fear is the latent, unchosen emotion of deserted peoples. Water, food, and fear were constantly on the minds, hearts, and stomachs of those early desert wanderers described in the Bible. The narratives from Exodus to the book of Deuteronomy describe some ten rebellions by these desert wanderers, mostly around their fear of dying in the desert without food and water. In evoking these most primal human sentiments, the Sinai desert, like so many other landscapes of Scripture, might rightly be described as "a psychological atlas" of early Israel.

Desert Pilgrimage

Once, Father Carl Trutter, a sixty-eight-year-old priest, and I set off on a three-day trip to Mt. Sinai. We had our gear, lots of water, sack lunches, and a small rental car—air-conditioning being our only requirement. Since the tank was only about half-full when we picked up the car at the Egyptian border, the attendant told us we would have to fill up at the first gas station we came to, some 30 miles away. So off we set on our desert pilgrimage, full throttle into the barren wilderness before us. We passed very few, if any, other vehicles until our first stop, the gas station in nowhere. The gas attendant came out and informed us apologetically that they were out of gas. "Out of gas! At a gas-station?" Now, I knew we were literally in the middle of nowhere. I felt a primal surge of fear tingle up my spine. Now what? Turn back? Go on? We guessed that we had enough gas to make it to the next promised station, so off we went. We got our gas. Awhile later we stopped the car for some sightseeing along the way. When we got back in the car, it wouldn't start. Again, the impulse of fear was almost immediate. What were we going to do in the middle of 24,000 square miles of nothing in 100 degree heat? I lifted the hood mostly to gain some sense of control over our circumstance, though not really having a clue as to what to do once the hood was up. Still, it wouldn't start. In a moment of inspiration, I took off my shoe and hit the battery cable as Moses might have hit the rock in this very same desert. Wal-lah! The car started and off we went.

In less than thirty-six hours, I had gained a deep appreciation for the fears and complaints and misery of our spiritual forebears who had been forced by God to wander a full generation in what seemed at first to be the God-forsaken Sinai desert. When your god is self-reliance (or even reliance on the modern convenience of an air-conditioned rental car, gas, food, or water even), the Sinai, in a blink could show such reliance to be a mirage. Certainly now, even three thousand years later, the words of Moses to his Sinai congregation ring so true to the psychological and spiritual geography of the desert (Deut. 8:2): "Remember the long way that the LORD your God has led you these forty years in the wilderness, in order to humble you, testing you to know what was in your heart." Certainly after our experience, I could more fully appreciate his warning, later restated by Jesus in his battle with his own desert demons, that all this happened "in order to make you understand that one does not live by bread alone, but by every word that comes from the mouth of the LORD" (8:3; Matt. 4:4; Luke 4:4). In a sense, the desert experience was and still is a test, an extreme test, in answering the age-old, primal question, "In what or whom do you believe?"

Scattered throughout the Sinai desert, to this day, are tiny little white chapels, some a thousand years old or more, in which pilgrims of long ago came to take the test of faith uttered by God through Moses. These early Christian monks were called hermits from the Greek word, *eremites*, which means, "one who lives in the desert." Paradoxically, they came to the god-forsaken barren desert, sometimes living in complete isolation for years, in order to find God. The desert is known, not just as the home of desert demons like Azazel of Old Testament fame (Lev. 16:10) or the *Diabolos* of New Testament fame (Matt. 4; Luke 4), but also as the place where God is revealed and God's word is heard. Even, Mohammed an early devotee of the Bible, spent weeks at a time in a desert cave outside Mecca where he eventually heard what he believed to be the word of God.

Presumably, God could have given the children of Israel the Ten Commandments anywhere on earth. Certainly, many more lovely spots come to mind. Yet, God chose Mt. Sinai in one of the most barren places in the desert of Sinai. Perhaps, God knew that only here would God's people be hot enough, tired enough, hungry enough, thirsty enough, utterly dependent, and sufficiently alert to actually hear the life-giving words of God. If silence is a hallmark of the desert, then God chose this place, faraway from every commotion and distraction to speak the words of salvation to those now able to truly hear them.

Shema: Listen!

In the utter silence of the desert, the book of Deuteronomy records that Moses spoke the words that would become the holiest words in Jewish faith (Deut. 6:4-7). As if to say, "Shhh! Quiet! Not a word! Silence! Listen!" Moses spoke, "Hear, O Israel; the LORD our God, the LORD is One. Love the LORD your God with all your heart with all your soul and with all your might." These words are called, for short, the *Shema* (Hebrew meaning, "Hear!" or better, "Listen!"). The words of the *Shema* are the glue that holds the book of Deuteronomy together, and as Jesus later suggests, they are the centrifugal force of *every* word, commandment, and story in the entire Bible. They are the magnet words around which the rest of the words of Scripture like iron shavings cling. The very first word, "Listen!" is proclaimed by Moses some twenty-six times throughout the book of Deuteronomy. It's as if he wants to call a moratorium on all lesser babblings—even his own. Before anything else is heard, before his words are recorded for all future generations, he wants all who are in the presence of his message to stop, quiet down our minds, cease every utterance, and listen!

The Jewish faithful have recited the words of the *Shema* for twenty-five centuries in their morning and evening prayers. The words of the *Shema* to stop and listen are among the very first words taught to Jewish children and the last spoken by elderly Jews in their dying breath. For Jews, these words are the center of life's gravity. They are written on tiny scrolls and rolled up and placed inside tiny decorative containers called *mezuzot* and attached to the doorposts of almost every Jewish home, or in offices, banks, bus stations, and other facilities. If you visit the McDonald's in Jerusalem today, even there, you find these words inside a *mezuzah*. For many Jews, the custom is to touch these words each and every time they enter or leave a building, a constant reminder to "Listen!"

Aristeas, a Jewish romance author writing during the time of Ptolemy II in the first century before the Common Era, imaginatively describes how the whole sacrificial system of the Second Temple was run in complete silence. This would have been quite a feat given the seven hundred priests officiating the almost round-the-clock slaughtering and heaving and loading and unloading, alongside those many others bringing the animals for sacrifice, washing down the floors after the sacrifices and disposing of the remains. Still, Aristeas recounts how even though the work was unrewarding, the priests did so with great joy. More surprisingly, he concludes without acknowledging any hyperbole, "everything was done with awe and reverence . . . so great is the silence everywhere that one would suppose there was no one in the place." Though clearly exaggerating his claims, Aristeas wanted to emphasize that silence was the first order of worship for the people of God. In his retelling, they understood the first words of the *Shema* quite literally. "Listen!"

We could all do with such a reminder. The average person speaks well over four thousand words a day and we are constantly bombarded with far more words and sounds and noise than that. In the modern industrialized world we are trapped in webs of sound from canned laughter on sitcoms to pagers to commercials overheard in traffic to white noise piped through our air vents at work. As Mark Slouka has suggested in his article entitled "Listening for Silence" (*Harpers Magazine*, April 1999), "everywhere drifts the aural refuse of our age." One reason why God may not seem to be appearing to us more frequently is because we are more into transmitting than we are receiving. A luncheon conversation with a friend led her to interrupt a monologue: "You simply aren't hearing me," she said. "You're transmitting fine, but your receiver is not working." How many of us have the same problem?

If God required the absolute silence of the desert in the off-chance that God's people might finally stop to listen, how much more do we, plagued by the noises of modernity, need to recapture a desert-like quiet, what Sue Kidd calls, "a concentrated stillness," if we ever hope to hear the voice of God today? When it comes to getting God's attention, we more often act like our ancient Roman counterparts who imagined that the best way to encounter the gods was by harassing and pestering the divinities with a flood of words. They called it, *fatigare deos*, meaning literally to "fatigue God" with our loud repetitious praises. We want to complain and grumble and cajole God into revealing truth. We are into loudness, hearing big voices. Give us a lightning bolt of truth, O God, and we will hear.

We Want Thunder

Elijah once fled to Mt. Sinai hoping to hear God speak to him as God had spoken so clearly to Moses there. I know the feeling. Like so many others, I too had made the arduous climb to the top of Mount Sinai in the middle of the night hoping that I might encounter the awesome presence of God at sunrise. On my way to the summit, in between the small kiosks set up by Bedouins to sell water and other treats, I was struck by the utter silence of my surroundings. I heard nothing but my own labored breathing. But Mt. Sinai can be a noisy place. Because of its height, Mt. Sinai attracts clouds like a magnet and is known for its temperamental storms. Many a hiking tourist finds the frigid cold and sudden storms of Mt. Sinai a dangerous surprise given its setting in the middle of the deadly hot desert. I was grateful that I took the advice of my guide, against all evidence of the hundred degree heat at the base of Mt. Sinai, to take with me a warm jacket. I nearly froze when I reached the summit, shivering so much that my pious plan to read Scripture, meditate, and pray on God's holy mountain to hear God's voice turned into a bit of a farce. One could easily imagine thunder and lightning crashing through the cloud-covered peaks, though no such storm conjured itself on this particular night. I imagined that Elijah, like so many before and since, had trudged up these steep paths hoping for an awesome encounter with the God of Moses. No doubt he was inspired by the same story that inspired me, a story that had been handed down to him over the course of hundreds of years of telling. At the summit, his experience also fell short of his expectations.

My guide-book identified a cave, now turned into a small sanctuary, to be the place where Elijah discovered God in a most unusual way. I imagined Elijah sitting in this cave in the middle of one of Mt. Sinai's awesome thunderstorms. I imagined his anticipation of hearing God speak to him in the thunder. I imagined his fear, his excitement, when the mighty winds split the mountain side and shattered the rocks round about. I've sat through some of California's earthquakes and seen the forest fires at close range in nearby mountains. I imagined Elijah sitting in the cave feeling the earth shake and watching the forest around him burn wildly wondering if he had stepped into the fiery presence of the Almighty. Was God about to speak to him as God had spoken to Moses so long ago on this very mountain? But, it wasn't to be. After the storm had died down, after the last quake had shaken, after the howling winds ceased, God spoke, but not as Elijah had expected. God whispered to Elijah in what some biblical translations call a "still small voice." Perhaps, a better translation would be, God spoke to him in "a thin voice of silence" (1 Kings 19:11-12).

How like Elijah, so many of us are. We want thunder. But like Elijah, we need silence. Before we can understand the word God speaks to us, we must learn to hear its absence. The Psalmist prays, "Truly my soul waits silently for God" (Ps. 62:2). Perhaps, should we ever manage to quiet ourselves long enough to hear God speak to us, we would discover that our boisterous efforts to encounter God reveal our deeper fears—that of actually hearing God's voice. In this too, we have historical precedents. The people of God in Exodus and Deuteronomy, unlike Elijah and modern tourists making the trek up the mountain, were not too anxious about hearing God's voice. The Hebrew nomads begged Moses to be their mediator when they first heard God's voice in the thunder, fire, and darkness on Mount Sinai (Deut. 5:25): "if we hear the voice of the Lord our God any longer, we shall die. For who is there of all flesh that has heard the voice of the living God speaking out of fire, as we have, and remained alive?" Later they concluded (Deut. 18:16), "Let us not hear the voice!" The desert voice of God, like the desert itself, can provoke fear in us, especially those of us who approach God too casually with our wordiness or are simply afraid of the silent void once we stop talking.

Later prophets, like Moses and Elijah, learned to hear God in "concentrated silence." Recall Ezekiel? Rabbi David Wolpe in his book, *In Speech and In Silence*: *The Jews Quest for God*, reminds readers that after eating the scroll of revelation, God ties Ezekiel's tongue (3:26). God does not open Ezekiel's mouth again for thirty chapters. Only then,

Ezekiel is finally able to say "thus God opened my mouth and I was no longer speechless" (33:22). Ezekiel was first taught strength in silence, and only then did he speak. Listening was serious business for the prophets and people of God, then and now. We sometimes need to have our tongues tied or be silenced by an encounter with the fearsome desert God.

Desert silence can be utterly dreadful because in the desert we approach the edge of all understanding. We are out-of-control there. The philosopher Wittgenstein once said, "The limits of [our] language are the limits of our words. To go beyond the limits of our world, to go beyond our understanding, to go beyond our human capacity for knowing, nothing but silence is called for." The people of God "trembled" before Mt. Sinai because they had reached the extreme limits of their words, their understanding, their human capacity, and nothing but silence was called for. The writer of Ecclesiastes would later summarize what must have been their feelings (5:1-2), "to draw near [to God] to listen is better than the sacrifice of fools . . . never be rash with your mouth, nor let your heart be quick to utter a word before God, for God is in heaven, and you are upon the earth; therefore let your words be few." Or to put it differently, St. Francis of Assisi said, "Preach, and if you must, use words." When Moses invites us repeatedly in the book of Deuteronomy to "Listen!" he invites us to relive the dreadful silence of the desert. He invites us into speechless awe. The first lesson of the *Shema* is to listen: "Hear, O Israel." "Be silent, O Israel!" "Listen!" "Shhh!"

God Is One

Now that God has their attention and ours, what Moses says next can truly be heard: "Hear O Israel. The LORD our God, the LORD is One." Likely as not, this declaration was an attempt to oppose the reality of competing claims as to which god was superior. In almost all periods of Israel's history, the worship of more than one god was a constant temptation. Up until this second sermon of Moses, God had been known in the narratives by means of a variety of manifestations. Various names or titles were used to speak of God or the gods including, God of your fathers, God of various locales, *El Roi*, *El Shaddai*, and so on. Even later in Canaan, God's identity would be at risk competing with the likes of Dagan and Baal and Asherath. Certainly, many of Israel's kings, even some of the best, for political expediency allowed the worship of other gods, sometimes even setting up alternative statues within the great Temple complex. So the LORD's identity was constantly at stake.

Deuteronomy is a crossroads book when even God's identity is at stake. Identity is always at risk between generational shifts, when the old ways give way to the new. A major concern for Moses, preaching to this new generation, was the identity of the God who brought them out of Egypt and promised them a glorious future in a new land. After forty years of wandering in the wilderness, living between the old story of God saving them from slavery and the promise of land still somewhere off in their unknown future, the people might well wonder whether the God they worshiped was up to the task.

A central theme, if not *the* central theme, in the book of Deuteronomy, then, is an attempt at persuading its readers in this and all future generations that the God of their salvation, the God of their worship, is not only God above all other gods, but even more significantly, is the one and only God. Such a confession might best be understood as "practical monotheism" in that it was an attempt to provide a rhetorical criterion for assessing the legitimacy of all present and future religious and political claims. Though Israel's ancient liturgies would, from the time of Moses on, always assert that the LORD was the only god that counted, it would only be after the severe lessons of the exile to Babylon, many years later, that this insight grew into unequivocal monotheism. In exile, the identity of God would once again be at stake. People would be tempted to worship the powerful gods of the empire. Isaiah's disciples (Isa. 45:14) articulate the sentiment of the *Shema*, perhaps better than at any time previously, when they proclaim to the exiles in Babylon, "With you alone is God, and he has no rival: there is no other god."

The editors of the book of Deuteronomy are deliberate in placing the *Shema* in chapter 6. As we have seen, chapter 5, the first "Hear O Israel" section, is basically a repeat of the Ten Commandments from the Book of the Covenant in Exodus. Within the first commandment, a warning about the exclusive worship of God is articulated in negative terms, "You shall *not* make for yourself an idol . . . you shall *not* bow down to them or worship them." The *Shema* captures the spirit of the first commandment by stating it positively: "The LORD our God, the Lord is One. You shall love the LORD your God with all your heart, will all your soul, with all your might."

Chapters 7 through 11 of the book of Deuteronomy have been described by Dennis Olson as expansions by Moses of the first commandment and the *Shema*. Moses details what practical effect belief in the LORD as the one and only God might have. The god of power is addressed in chapter 7 by arguing against making power politics your god. Trusting in nations mightier and more numerous than emergent Israel, trusting in their mighty gods, is to polytheize. Stress is placed in this chapter on the singular power of Yahweh, who alone is warrior and defender of emergent Israel. Chapter 8 serves as a warning against making material possessions the object of one's worship. Even good and necessary things like water and food should not be given ultimate worth because, "one does not live by bread alone" (8:3). Moses reminds his congregation that the whole while they wandered in the desert, their clothes and shoes didn't wear out. God provided for them. Furthermore, if and when they some day become wealthy, they must not imagine their gain was simply due to their own power and strength. They must always worship the Giver without forgetting the gift. Chapters 9 and 10 are a warning against making oneself God. The concern here is self-righteousness, thinking that God has called them and promised them land because of their moral decency or inherent goodness. Moses spends these fifty-two verses outlining their utter humanity, lest they be tempted to imagine themselves god-like. And finally, chapter 11 repeats the language of the *Shema*, particularly underscoring the positive call to love the one and only God with all one's heart, soul, and might.

Moses wished to convey the glorious notion that in confessing that there was one and only God was good news, indeed. Over and above and through a chaotic, divided, mixed-up reality as we all experience it, there remains an even greater unity—a coherence, a meaningfulness, a purpose. Furthermore, to confess that the LORD God is One, singular, is to confess that over and above and through all the many laws that can be written and followed (or not), even over and above and beyond the updated-soon-to-need-updating-again laws of Deuteronomy, there is Integrity, Wholeness, and Completeness in God: the one and only.

Such a singular, unified view of reality has a totalizing effect, even at times, a totalitarian danger to it. In Deuteronomy, the downside of such a totalizing view of God does lead Moses to argue that God can and does ask the people of God to devote to him all their enemies in holy war. This same totalitarian, all-encompassing view of God, inasmuch as people claim this God as their god exclusively, has led to religious wars throughout history. At the same time, if God is one, then to claim God exclusively as one's own is the height of arrogance. Reality is relativized by the one and only God, so that any projection of one's own narrow, violent, parochial, denomi(national) god onto the universe comes perilously close to disobeying the first commandment. As will be discussed in a later chapter, even Moses' claims about God are subject to a new response, a new reading, a rewrite, a nuanced interpretation, as subject to the One and only God. One of those responses would come twelve hundred years later in Christ, a Moses-like leap away from a violent Mosaic monotheism.

The Greatest Law Is Love

If the *Shema* is concerned about getting our full attention and defending God's unique status as God, it is equally concerned to defend the only or ultimate feeling worthy of God, the feeling of love. When Jesus was approached by some scribes squabbling over which was the greatest of all the laws of the Old Testament (Mark 12:28-34), Jesus simply quoted the *Shema* in arguing that to love God with all one's heart, soul, and might was the greatest law of all. Rabbi Akiba, the most influential teacher of his day early in the second century after Christ, suffered martyrdom along with 850,000 other Jews in revolt against the Roman empire. As his flesh was torn from his body with iron tongs, he could be heard reciting this portion of the *Shema*: "Hear O Israel. The LORD our God, the LORD is one. Love the LORD with all your heart and soul and might."

How is such love imaginable? Without a doubt, this command to love God with all one's heart, soul, and might, must have come after the people had experienced God's love for themselves. The book of Deuteronomy understands Israel's relationship to God as that of a son (Deut. 8:5; 14:1) which suggests a bond of love like that of moms and dads and their children. Much later, the apostle John in the New Testament (1 John 4:19) borrows from Deuteronomy (10:15) to describe how such love of God might be imagined, "We love, because God first loved us." A relational God like the God of Abraham, the God of the Exodus, the God of the Mosaic Covenant, certainly allows for a whole variety of feelings toward God, not unlike that of the variety of feelings between parents and their children. For desert wanderers, fear of the desert-God was certainly one of those possible feelings. We're told that the people "trembled" when they approached the Mountain of God. But here in the *Shema*, all feelings, including fear, are made relative to the unique stress it places on loving God.

Defining our relationship with God as one of love is a distinctive contribution of Deuteronomy. So much has been written and said by mostly Christian readers down through the ages, that the God of the Old Testament is a mean-spirited ogre. Marcion, a new Christian in the second century after Christ, went so far as to suggest that the God of the Old Testament was an altogether different God than the God of the New Testament. So much so, that Marcion argued for a Christian Bible without an Old Testament. He wondered aloud how anyone could love such a god portrayed in the Old Testament who was anything but loving. Never mind that God's just vengeance for disobedience in Deuteronomy 6:9 is overshadowed by God's overwhelming love a verse later (6:10) by a ratio of five hundred to one.

In Deuteronomy, God's love, like all true love is no sappy, sentimental love, though it is endearing. Deuteronomy stresses covenant love, treaty loyalty, love-with-obligation. For Moses, loving God is as specific as loving others, especially the poor, stranger, and orphan (10:18, 19). The Great Commandment of Jesus about loving such a loving God with our whole selves echoes the words of the *Shema*. Immediately after inviting Israel to love God so completely, the rest of the book of Deuteronomy invites its readers to love others as well in legislation that envisions the Great Society.

Jesus spoke of this Deuteronomic turn as the second greatest commandment, "to love our neighbor as ourselves." The form of this second great commandment is found in Deuteronomy, chapters 12-28. In these chapters Moses defines what it means to love God and each other in practice, not just theory. In essence, he simply provides laws that coincide with and elaborate on the remaining nine commandments. As will be addressed in the next chapter, these ordinances and laws in chapters 12-28 might be called the social extension of the Great Commandment. They are concerned about living together and loving each other as neighbors. Is it any wonder that Jesus, when referring to the *Shema*, argued that upon it all the laws and the prophets hung (Matt. 22:40)? Indeed, Jesus must have known that quite literally, the structure and the theological outlook of the whole book of Deuteronomy hangs on the *Shema*'s invitation to love God. Such a love relationship emerges from listening to the voice of love that speaks from the silent desert void.

CHAPTER FIVE

Between Life and Death

"Now, there are many millions who in their sects and churches feel the order, 'Do thou,' and throw their weight into obedience. And there are millions more who feel predestination in 'Thou shalt.' Nothing they may do can interfere with what will be. But 'Thou mayest'! Why, that makes a man great, that gives him stature with [God], for in his weakness and his filth . . . he has still the great choice."
—John Steinbeck, East of Eden

Read Deuteronomy 12-30

You have a God-given absolute right to disobey Scripture. In fact, some Scripture must be disobeyed. For example, were you to conclude that what I just said might lead some people away from God, then I would surely invite you to disobey Deuteronomy 13:6, 10, which reads in part, "If anyone entices you away from God . . . stone him to death!" Please don't obey this commandment. With few exceptions, you and I do not *have* to do anything. We certainly don't have to obey the Ten Commandments. We don't have to obey the many statutes and ordinances outlined in the law codes of Deuteronomy 12-30. And, in many instances, we don't. The reader should expect some clarification here, especially since Moses' third sermon in the book of Deuteronomy allows for no exceptions to a strict obedience of the laws written therein.

As was noted in chapter 1, many commentators argue that the laws of Deuteronomy 12-28 were those found in a scroll by the young King Josiah when he undertook a renovation of the temple. Be that as it may, Moses concludes this body of laws with his third desert sermon in chapters 29-30. After cataloging law after law outlining his vision of the Great Society in Chapters 12-28, Moses gathers together anyone and everyone who is still alive, from the least to the greatest, for a grand covenant renewal ceremony. The crowd includes the nobility, the leaders, the tribal chiefs, the elders, and officials. We would expect that. But the gathered ones also include all the men, women, children, even the common laborers (Deut. 29:10-11). What's more, Moses reminds them that the covenant about to be renewed is the same covenant God swore to uphold for their ancestors. But more than that, this covenant is for all those gathered before him on the desert plains and, significantly, also for "those who are not here with us today" (29:13-14). In other words, God, through Moses' sermonizing, invites a response to the covenant renewal service from all future readers, including all of us who understand ourselves as people of faith today.

The Crossroads of Life and Death

The book of Deuteronomy is Scripture at the crossroads of life and death. So too, this final sermon of Moses marks off choices that vitally matter. Like all decisions made in the desert, each decision can mean the difference between dying or living. The desert is unforgiving. Moses confronts his listeners with one of the most explicit calls for decision in the Bible: to choose to obey or disobey the commandments and laws of God. Moses puts it bluntly (30:19): "I have set before you life and death, blessings and curses. Choose life so that you and your descendents might live." The either/or language used by Moses is crossroads language, boundary language—the kind of language natural for a book some-where between wilderness wandering and settling down, between promise and fulfillment, between the generations, between Israel's adolescence and maturity. When we were children in Sunday school, we used to sing a song that captures the essence of decision-making described here. Whereas we sang it with respect to our decision to follow Christ, it also applies to the decisions here called for by Moses. The refrain for the people in the wilderness would go something like this, "I met [Moses] at the crossroads, where the two ways meet. . . ." The call of Moses is the call of freedom to choose which of two roads to take. My own experience in traveling through the Sinai desert, where we frequently came to unmarked intersections in the middle of nowhere, suggests the gravity of decisions made at crossroads. Deciding which road to take, or not to take, could very well have meant the difference between arriving at our destination or getting utterly and terribly lost. For people of the desert, the consequences expressed by Moses' use of the language of "blessing" and "cursing" is not at all exaggerated. Obey and live! Disobey and die!

Like the whole book of Deuteronomy, Moses preaches using the ancient treaty covenant form to structure his sermon. In the two previous chapters (27-28), he describes the kinds of activities that will evoke a curse and the ugly consequences that will come upon those who are accursed. The tally of death includes: disease, pestilence, drought, famine, destruction, loss of real estate and possessions, slander, psychological disorders, and exile to name a few. A shorter more pleasant tally of blessings for all those who obey includes: fertility in the field and in the womb, increased numbers of livestock, more real estate holdings, protection from enemy attack, and, for former slaves, a wonderful promotion in status that they will stand above all other nations on earth.

Other covenant renewal ceremonies reported in Scripture, like the ones in Exodus 19:3-9 or Joshua 24:15-24, are straightforward narrative accounts of these events that happened sometime in the past. In those reports, we, the readers, are told that the people in those renewal services responded positively and recommitted themselves to God again. Here in Deuteronomy, however, we, the readers, never find out what choices the people gathered before Moses make. We are never told by the narrator the outcome. Why the difference in reporting? It may have to do with the liturgical nature of the book of Deuteronomy. For Moses and the narrator of Deuteronomy, the gathered congregation included not just those surrounding Moses "at that time," but also includes all subsequent believers gathered around the text even now. For those "at that time" standing on the banks of the Jordan River, their whole future stood open before them. How they chose to follow the teachings set out before them by Moses could very well determine their destinies. So also it is true for us. We, like our ancient forebears of faith, do not yet know our own futures. Through a liturgical retelling of the covenant renewal ceremony, the writers of Deuteronomy include us in the hour of decision faced by all those waiting to cross the Jordan. The "there and then" becomes the "here and now" which becomes the "not yet" in each retelling and reenactment of the story.

We Have No Excuses

Here's the rub! Moses expects not only his contemporary congregation to obey *all* the statutes and commandments that the LORD gave to them, but he also expects us to obey *all* the same statutes and commandments (Deut. 30:8): "obey the LORD, observing *all* his commandments that I [Moses] am commanding you this day." Moses does not exempt anyone who would claim to be part of the believing community from keeping *all* the commandments given by God in the book of Deuteronomy. The prophets Jeremiah and Ezekiel claim that keeping the commandments is actually possible with a change of heart (Jer. 31:33; Ezek. 11:19-20). Could it be they got this so-called "advanced understanding" of the law from the book of Deuteronomy itself? Foreshadowing these claims, Moses says (Deut. 30:6,8), "The LORD your God will circumcise your heart and the heart of your descendants, so that you will love the LORD your God with all your heart and with all your soul, in order that you may live . . . then you shall obey the LORD, observing *all* his commandments that I am commanding you today." Then as if to solidify his claim that these demands are not impossible, he continues (Deut. 30:12-14), "This commandment . . . is not too hard for you, nor is it too far away. It is not in heaven that you should say, 'Who will go up to heaven for us and get it for us so that we may hear it and observe it?' Neither is it beyond the sea, that you should say, 'Who will cross to the other side of the sea for us so that we may hear it and observe it?' No, the word is very near you; it is in your mouth and in your heart for you to observe." That is to say, you have no excuses! We have no excuses! Obey or disobey, but choose this day whom to serve.

So far so good. The laws in Deuteronomy are remarkable in their scope. The fact that many of these laws expand their earlier versions in Exodus in more generous ways then the originals, suggests a growing concern for what later generations might call "equal protections under the law." There is in Deuteronomy a movement toward a more "democratic spirit." As mentioned elsewhere, the laws of Deuteronomy provide a trajectory in the direction of the Great Society. Laws having to do with institutional forms of governance form the core of Deuteronomy's law code. In a real sense, Deuteronomy has many of the markings of a Constitution of sorts, containing laws regulating municipal judges (16:18-20), limiting the power of the king (17:14-20), circumscribing the privileges and duties of the priesthood (18:1-8), guiding the prophetic guild (18:15-22), providing rules of proper conduct in warfare (20:1-20) and so on. There are laws protecting a person's security (5:17; 24:7; 27:18), guarding against slander and false accusations (Deut. 5:20; 19:15-21), protecting women from sexual harassment (21:10-14; 24:1-5). Some laws provide unprecedented dignity for free men and women and, most notably, protection against exploitation of their servants (15:12-18). Real estate agents would appreciate the good inheritance laws (25:5-10) and property protections (5:19; 22:1-4; 25:13-15) found here. There are labor laws guaranteeing a worker a decent living (24:14; 25:4), family and social laws securing marriage covenants (5:18; 22:13-20), and laws protecting orphans, widows, and the poor from exploitation (23:19; 24:6,12-15,17; 27:18). Lawyers might appreciate the laws guaranteeing access to free trials and legal services (1:17; 10:17-18; 16:18-20; 17:8-13; 19:15-21). Environmentalists and animal rights advocates would approve of the laws that protect animals from cruelty and the caution against the exploitation of the environment (22:4, 6-7; 25:4). And, of course, the Ten Commandments themselves (5:6-21) which serve to introduce all these other laws and are rightly considered the foundation of all subsequent jurisprudence and the greatest summary of law known to humankind. Deuteronomy is a marvelous piece of legislation, indeed!

Most of us, in principle at least, can agree that obeying such a wonderful set of laws as listed is quite noble. For the most part, we readily and gladly would and do obey these laws. In fact, many of these very laws have been embedded in the constitutions of most democratic countries today.

But what about those laws in Deuteronomy that aren't so life-affirming? What about laws against crosscultural marriage (7:3) or laws calling for the annihilation of those who don't follow Israel's God (7:5)? How do connoisseurs of pork chops, spareribs, lobster or steak cooked rare feel about laws forbidding these tasty dishes (12:15)? How about laws that demand the stoning of heretics (6:10), disobedient children (21:18-21), and adulterers (22:15-30)? Or laws excluding the handicapped from entering the worship service (23:1-6)? These laws too are part of the covenant of which Moses demands a choice regarding our obedience. All these laws fall under his call of obedience, to "Choose this day, life or death, blessing or curse." So which laws are we to obey to avoid the curse? Which laws do we follow to gain blessing? Surely not *all* of them.

For all of us who like to run to the Old Testament law selectively to find some accusation against a certain sin or vice, we must stop and ask ourselves, why this sin and not that? Why stone the homosexual and not the disobedient child? Why curse the adulterer and not the handicapped church visitor? A grave dilemma arises in our selectivity of this or that law. For those laws that we dislike, or rightfully consider inhumane, we argue against them using the criteria of "cultural limitation," or try to discount them as "ceremonial" or simply because they are "Old" Testament law. By contrast, laws we find favorable are often supported with claims as to their "transcultural nature." The good laws, we say, are "universal and timeless." The bad laws are "particular and time-bound."

We are often ready to affirm the great Ten Commandments as universally applicable, even though in many respects they are quite culturally limited. For example, the tenth commandment about coveting, says nothing about a covetous wife. Neither Moses himself, nor the book of Deuteronomy, anywhere distinguishes between the Ten Commandments and the rest of the laws in Deuteronomy when we are commanded to follow *all* of them for our blessing. What's a Bible-believing person to do? Obey this law and hope for blessing, while disobeying that law and fear being cursed?

The Principle of Free Choice

In answering these questions, let's step back from the specifics and look, first of all, at the principle Moses and the book of Deuteronomy seem to be sharing with us. We'll return to specific laws in a bit. For Moses, and apparently for God, a very basic principle is at stake—the God-given absolute freedom of choice. Such a choice is so fundamental to a biblical view of humanity's relationship with God that it is surprising how we spend our lives trying to avoid the radical nature of that God-given freedom. From Adam and Eve to you and me we'd rather pass the buck of freedom, especially when we choose wrongly. We pass the buck of freedom to each other, to the Serpent, to the legislature, to our parents, even to God. The freedom of the desert is hard. It suffers wrong choices ruthlessly. To take a turn down the wrong desert pathway could mean the difference between life and death for us and for others. And so we fear our freedom. We hate it at times. We avoid it at others. Often, we refuse to accept such responsibility. But, always, always, the freedom God gives includes the absolute freedom to choose rightly or wrongly, to obey or to disobey, in spite of our fears.

The very structure of the Torah (Genesis–Deuteronomy) begins in the garden of Eden and ends on the banks of the Jordan River, bookended, as it were, by human choice. God's first encounter with humanity was to offer them real choices of real consequence. It's also telling to see that among God's last words to Moses in the book of Deuteronomy, after again giving the people real choices of real consequence, are these, "I shall hide my face from them. I shall see what their end will be" (31:17-18; 32:20). It is as if God steps back to see if the people of God standing on the banks of the Jordan River might make better choices than their originating parents did in the Garden. Such a deliberate placement of these stories of human choice at the beginning and end of the Torah establishes the primary theological principle that God created humans with the real power of decision. Men and women were created with the ability to oppose God's will.

Immediately after the Torah story, the Former Prophets (Joshua–2 Kings) tell the story of the people crossing the Jordan River, entering the Promised Land, only to end up at the end of the account being carted into exile. Placed as it is in the second part of the Hebrew canon and immediately after the open-ended, choice-laden future of the Torah, it seems clear that the compilers of Scripture wanted to illustrate the (negative) choices made by emergent Israel that would explain how they eventually ended up where they did. Now, once again, years later, the exiles in Babylon found themselves on the banks of another river, the Euphrates River, looking back across its stormy banks to the Promised Land. The end of the Former Prophets (2 Kings) is not unlike the end of the

Torah itself (Deuteronomy). Once again, the pilgrim people of God find themselves standing on the banks of this other river. They are compelled to confront a future that will determine their destinies. Will they get to return to Judah from their exiled existence? How might their choices now effect their future destinies?

The third section of the Hebrew canon, called the Writings, reiterates the importance Scripture gives to the principle of human choice. The Wisdom traditions, in particular, confirm the trust God has in the reasoning power of humans to gain wisdom by means of trial and error necessitated by freedom of choice. In the book of Proverbs, for example, we find back-to-back proverbs that explicitly contradict each other (Prov. 24:4-5). The assumption of the book of Proverbs appears to be that if a child is brought up in wisdom of the LORD, as illustrated in the first nine chapters, then he should be capable of discerning which proverb is appropriate for which circumstance. One might extend this wisdom principle to the whole of Scripture with its many different and sometimes conflicting theological viewpoints. Scripture doesn't do the work of discernment for us, we must do so ourselves. Scripture does not choose which laws are best obeyed for our own setting. We are required to choose wisely among the biblical options available to us.

Even the rabbis get in on the fundamental principle at stake here. In the Talmud, the rabbinic commentary on the Bible, two conflicting points of view are held on the nature of the freedom given by God to God's people. One set of rabbis argues that when God gave the law to Moses on Mt. Sinai, God held the whole mountain over the heads of the people saying, "If you do not accept my Torah, here will be your graves." In effect, God cajoled, nagged, and worse, threatened, Israel into obedience. The other set of rabbis argues simply that God offered the Torah to all other nations, each turned it down after reviewing what was in it. Only Israel voluntarily accepted the burden of the law because the blessings that come with being in intimate relationship with God were far greater than any burden. Of course, the Talmud, in good rabbinic fashion, seems to favor majority opinion, but not always. Sometimes nothing is completely resolved. In cleverness, that choice is left to the discernment of future readers. More choices!

The Flexibility of Discernment

Certainly, the "people of the way" as the Jewish followers of Jesus were first called, initially never intended to stop following any of the Old Testament laws. But as the message of Christ spread to the non-Jewish world, questions arose about whether it was necessary for these converts to be circumcised or to eat kosher or to keep other scriptural laws. Eventually, through some very difficult negotiations between the Jewish and Gentile followers of Christ most notably described as the Jerusalem Council in Acts 15, compromises were reached and decisions made that large chunks of the Scripture no longer necessarily applied to some of their new converts in this new situation. It had always been pointed out by Jesus that the original purpose of the law was to help people learn how to love each other and that should always be its true intent. This flexibility of discernment was crucial to the emergent church. It remains so today.

Outside of Scripture, in principle and practice, we seem to understand the role that human choice plays in deciding how best to live together. As suggested in chapter 3, we know that not all laws that remain on the books still require our obedience. Some laws have lost their relevance completely due to many factors, not least of which is the passage of time. We are free, in effect, to disobey those laws. It may be we need to grant ourselves the same prerogative when it comes to some of the laws in the Bible.

It may seem terrifying to make decisions of consequence by deciding which laws to obey and which are no longer necessary to obey. Such radical freedom could seem to encourage moral and civil anarchy. And it has. However, our fear of being wrong cannot lead us to ignore the principle modeled for us in the book of Deuteronomy. Even though Moses is arguing his own set of God-given laws, and even though Moses wants his readers to obey the laws he has just laid out, he does not ultimately undermine the greater principle of the absolute right to obey or disobey those very laws. The apostle Paul describes this potentially wild freedom by saying, "all things are lawful for me" (1 Cor. 6:12).

The simple scary troubling truth remains, as it always has and will, that every human has the vocation of decision-maker. Like it or not, we're stuck with this freedom. In principle, we are free to do anything, to disbelieve anything, to disobey every law. We are even free to relinquish our freedom of choice, which most of us do much of the time for better or worse. We can give up that freedom to a predestinarian, a cult leader, a Pope, a professor, an abusive spouse, a political dictator, or some other authority. Like wanderers in the wilderness of life, we'd rather not grow up or shoulder the burden of radical choice too soon. We prefer to do without the burden of deciding which laws on the books or in the Bible must still be obeyed for our blessing or judgment. Yet, to go from the wilderness wanderings to the "promised land," from adolescent faith to mature faith, those exact choices must be made. "Growing up is hard to do," as the song says. If the biblical covenant that serves to guide our relationship with God and others is to work, the principal of voluntary choice must remain central to the law becoming a blessing in our lives, less a burden, less so a curse. The words of Moses are just as true for us today as when they were spoken, at least these words of Moses, "I set before you life and death, blessing and curse." Choose.

The early Anabaptists of the sixteenth century believed in this radical biblical freedom. They defended to the death, their own deaths many times, the absolute right to dissent and disobey wrong laws. Certain laws were so tied to what was claimed to be biblical, Mosaic, even Christ-centered that to refuse to go along was deemed heretical. In those days, heretics were killed outright. The consequences of their

choices were often every bit as serious as the life-and-death
choices set before the refugees in the wilderness listening to the
three sermons of Moses. Yet, it was precisely the theological
principle of free choice that they believed was worth risking
death.

Freedom to Disobey

Ironically, in the act of putting before us a clear choice for
or against obedience, Moses opened the door to disobeying
some of the very laws he was defending. Such is our choice.
But is such radical freedom necessarily a moral and ethical
free-for-all? It can be and sometimes is the price God and we
pay for such a fundamental blessing. But our God-given
blessing of freedom need not become a license to sin more
boldly or to thumb our noses at authority or to individually
assemble our own little universe of laws only we will follow
and none other. Though the apostle Paul, knowing this
ancient tradition of freedom, did confess that "all things are
lawful" for him, he quickly adds, "but I will be mastered by
none." Though we have the absolute God-given right to disobey
even God's laws and statutes and ordinances, the test of our
character is what we do with this radical freedom. When
Moses commands his congregation to "choose life," twice he
defines such a life as loving God, walking in the ways of
God, and remaining steadfastly committed to God (30:16,
20). The real truth of the matter is that we are free, also, to
obey!

Wesley's Quadrilateral

With such freedom, how then might we go about picking
and choosing which laws, whether in the Old Testament or
the New Testament that are still worthy of our loving obedience? I know of no more adequate response to this question
which does justice to the model laid out for us in Scripture,
which fully accounts for the various expressions of Christian
community, which adequately conveys life as we live it, and
which underscores God's sovereign rights as creator, then

that which has been articulated by John Wesley, the great evangelist of the eighteenth century. What Wesley says is not new, it in fact is the process by which almost all decisions have been reached regarding our obedience to God from the days of Moses until now. The four principles which Wesley laid out, and have since been called his Quadrilateral, are: Scripture, tradition, reason, and experience. Each principle on its own is inadequate, though some believers have frequently used one to the neglect of the other. In Christian history, many Protestants have emphasized Scripture alone as wholly adequate for determining decisions facing us. But we have seen that Scripture alone doesn't always adjudicate these thorny issues for us. Indeed, Scripture sometimes exacerbates the problem by not offering a unified worldview or single theology between its covers. Roman Catholics have given preeminence to tradition, which for them usually means the decisions of the bishops, councils and Pope. This too creates difficulties with its narrow and hierarchical understanding of tradition. Pentecostals go heavy on experience, mainline Protestants on reason and on it goes. Wesley, though giving more weight to Scripture than all other categories, rightly cautioned against elevating any one of these principles to the place of God, since God is always a free agent and won't be boxed in by any one of them.

So we are advised in our decision-making process to use Scripture, first and foremost. In this sense, Scripture becomes its own self-correcting apparatus by offering up counterpoints of view that may challenge this or that understanding. Such expressions as "Scripture against Scripture," or "canon within the canon" are ways of taking into account how Scripture can assist in its own interpretation, while still doing justice to the freedom of choice we have as Scripture readers. But we can look for other help as well. We can take traditions (small "t," plural) into account. The interpretations and guidance of other people of faith down through the ages can assist us today. Here too, it is important to remember that some traditions have outgrown their usefulness. The whole

New Testament took the traditions of the Old Testament very seriously, in some cases heightening those traditions to make an important innovative point, in other cases sidelining some traditions as being no longer adequate to express the new thing God was doing at that time. Trusting our own experience can either mislead or lead us aright when balanced by the other criteria. The story of conflict resolution in Acts 15 provides one good example of how trusting in their own experience and the guidance of the Holy Spirit proved to be the right decision by the Jewish followers of Jesus. They came to a consensus about welcoming the newly minted Christian Gentiles into their fellowship and concluded, "God, who knows the human heart, testified to them by giving them the Holy Spirit, just as he did to us" (Acts 15:8). And then in a gracious letter to their fellow believers, they wrote (15:28), "For it seemed good to the Holy Spirit and *to us* to impose no further burden then these essentials upon you."

God also wants us to use our brains. As I once heard from a fellow pastor, "God didn't just make brains to amuse neurosurgeons. Use them." The Wisdom traditions of Scripture underscore the wonderful gift of human intelligence given to us for wise discernment. I caution against simply defining reason or rationality in terms of logical deduction or unemotional detachment, though those qualities are certainly important components of what it means to be people of reason. However, there can be a certain rationality in other forms of deduction as well. A growing appreciation for what some have called "emotional intelligence," "intuitive intelligence," or "kinesthetic intelligence" should be acknowledged. And then, also, whether or not one splits the body-mind connection between Wesley's categories of "experience" and "reason," it's important to allow for both as we enter the decision-making process.

As for the reasonableness of this or that set of laws, common sense can sometimes be a harbinger of good choices. Common sense is sometimes described as that quality we gain through common experience or by tapping into laws seemingly imbedded within us. Proverbs are a good example of common sense, the compressed wisdom of the ages. Some things we just know, with or without formal legislation. For example, many of us just know that the telephone never rings until you're settled in the bathroom. We just know that for every human reaction there is an overreaction or that there really is only one fruitcake in the world. We just know that if you actually look like your passport picture, you aren't well enough to travel or that the cost of living will always rise to exceed income. We just know it.

Common sense tells us that becoming a disciple of Jesus, being filled with the Spirit of Jesus, and imitating the life of Jesus might help us to just know how or whether to follow this or that command or law. Most importantly, we just know that Christ's criteria of "loving God and loving others" must play a part in all our choices for blessing. Whenever Jesus broke with the old laws about the Sabbath or ritual cleanness or fellowship with sinners, he always opted to do the loving thing over the legal thing. In John 10, Jesus deliberately chose to disobey the age-old Sabbath law in order to heal a paralytic man. This was no small disobedience. Some wanted to stone him to death for his disobedience and rightfully so, according to the law. After all, Sabbath law was established in creation itself. To disobey the Sabbath was tantamount to undermining the very fabric of the created order. Yet, when faced with the choice of obeying the law or not, Jesus chose disobedience so that the higher law of love would prevail. To be sure, Jesus never intended to completely overthrow the Sabbath laws, though the consequence of his act, if generalized, would surely do so. Indeed, the nearly complete failure among many Christians today to preserve the sanctity of Sabbath rest even in our Sunday observance, indicates the danger in generalizing a particular act of disobedience even for a higher good. Still, there may be specific times and particular circumstances in which even the best laws require a righteous disobedience in order for a greater healing to take place. One might imagine a situation in which it is better for two people to divorce even though Christ once said of marriage, "what God has joined together, let no one break asunder." If a relationship has become so toxic, so debilitating, so unhealthy, better to break the law of marriage, so that each partner may be healed. In doing so, no one must suggest that the law of marriage should be abolished or that in divorcing, a couple is not breaking the law of God. Rather, it is better simply to admit that in this or that particular case, breaking the law is justified so that healing might take place. Clearly, law and love are not mutually exclusive. We, however, with God's help and in due soberness, must decide what to do or what not to do when expressing love for God and for each other.

Timshel—"Thou Mayest"

Let us conclude this chapter by ending where we began. The quotation at the beginning of this chapter is actually that of Lee, the Chinese housekeeper of Adam Trask. Adam is one of the main characters in John Steinbeck's novel, *East of Eden,* a story that unfolds over two generations containing the great themes of the Bible story about Cain and Abel. Adam is one of two sons of Cyrus Trask living on a farm in Connecticut. His brother's name is Charles. The boys grow up with a special bond between them. On one of Cyrus's birthdays, his son Adam gives his father a stray puppy, while the other son, Charles, gives him an expensive Swiss Army knife. Cyrus never uses the knife, though takes a particular fondness for the puppy turned dog. To complicate the plot, after many years and a stint in the Cavalry, Adam returns home and falls in love with a former prostitute named Cathy, who had killed her own parents in a deliberately set house fire some years earlier. Cathy's past is unknown to the Trask family. Adam ends up marrying Cathy, who by now is pregnant by his brother Charles. The plot thickens.

Adam and Cathy buy a large farm in Salinas Valley, California, and hire the Chinese housekeeper named Lee.

Cathy gets pregnant again and delivers twin boys, who they name Caleb and Aron. Cathy's murderous ways emerge again when she tries to kill her husband Adam but botches the job, shooting him in the shoulder instead. She flees to a whorehouse and Adam, not wanting to see her in prison, covers for her, though he is devastated by her abandonment. Their sons, Aron and Cal, the twins, grow up not knowing anything of their mother. Many years later, Aron enters Stanford University one year early because of his giftedness, while Cal stays home and decides to work in the bean industry. At the same time, Cal decides that all the profits he makes from his hard work on the farm, he'll give to his aging father, who lost all of his money on a failed cabbage venture. One Thanksgiving, when Aron returns home from school on break, Cal presents his father with the hard earned $15,000 he had saved. Adam, the father, rejects the money and adds insult to injury by saying that the pride he gets from Aron's scholarly accomplishments are worth more to him than money. Weeping, Cal takes the money to his room and burns it. He vows revenge on Aron and does so by revealing to Aron something Cal had learned earlier but kept secret. He tells Aron that their mother is still alive all these years later and is still a working prostitute. Aron is so shocked he leaves Stanford and joins the army where he is killed in battle. Cal feels terribly guilty for Aron's death, as if he had pulled the trigger himself. When their father, Adam, hears the news of Aron's death, he goes into shock and soon thereafter dies. But before he dies, Cal goes to his father's bedside and asks him for forgiveness. His father, Adam, only mutters one word in response, "*timshel.*"

A reader of Hebrew would recognize in father Adam's final utterance to Cal, the warning God made to Cain regarding the power of sin just before Cain goes out to kill his brother Abel (Gen. 4:7b, *v'atah timshal ba*). John Steinbeck built his entire novel on understanding the meaning of this fragment of conversation. As English translations of this phrase suggest, the word *timshal/timshel* in Hebrew can be translated in various ways. The *New Revised Standard Version* translates the phrase as, "You must master it," making it a direct order from God. The *King James Version* translates the phrase as, "Thou shalt rule over him," implying a predestined outcome, leaving Cain little choice in the matter. On the other hand, the Hebrew phrase can very readily be understood as so many Jewish translations render the phrase, "You may rule over it." The full warning by God to Cain in the biblical account sounds reminiscent of the choices for good or evil that Moses puts before his desert congregation. God says, to Cain, "If you do well, will you not be accepted? And if you do not do well, sin is lurking at the door; its desire is for you, but you must/shall/may rule over it."

Are we responsible for our actions or not? Could Cain have made different choices than he did? Could Cal have chosen differently in his bitter, though understandable, response to his brother Aron? Can Moses dare hold his congregation responsible for choosing life or death, blessing or judgment? These are the kinds of questions Lee, the Chinese housekeeper wonders aloud about to his boss and friend Adam, father of Cal and Aron. Lee is struggling to decide on the best among the different options for translating the Hebrew word *timshel* in the Cain and Abel story, the very word that Adam would later utter in his dying breath. Lee continues the conversation with Adam regarding the difference between the "Thou shalts" and "Thou mayests" of life (see quotation in the heading). Lee decides that the correct translation can't be "thou shall" which would imply that Cain doesn't have to worry about sin "crouching at the door" because God said he "shall," that to say, he would eventually conquer sin. Such a translation would mean Cain could not be held responsible for his choice. On the other hand, translating the expression as "Thou mayest" implies, the choice is yours, you are responsible. All this pondering about the meaning of *timshel* brings Lee to conclude his thoughts on the human soul as being "a lovely and unique thing in the universe. It is always attacked

and never destroyed—because 'Thou mayest.'" Then he
clarifies,

> "'Thou mayest rule over sin,' Lee said. [Adam
> responds], 'That's it. I do not believe all men are
> destroyed. I can name you a dozen who were not, and
> they are the ones the world lives by. . . . Surely most
> men are destroyed, but there are others who like pillars
> of fire guide frightened men through the darkness.
> 'Thou mayest, Thou mayest!' What glory! It is true that
> we are weak and sick and quarrelsome, but if that is all
> we ever were, we would, millenniums ago, have disap-
> peared from the face of the earth. A few remnants of
> fossilized jawbone, some broken teeth in strats of lime-
> stone, would be the only mark man would have left of
> his existence in the world. But the choice, Lee, the
> choice of winning! I had never understood it or accepted
> it before. 'Thou mayest rule over sin!'"

In his third sermon in the book of Deuteronomy, Moses
invites, no demands, categorical obedience. Life and death
stand in the balance. Paradoxically, his demand to choose
between life and death, stated in stark either/or choices,
argues, in fact, for the right to disobey for the sake of life. In
defending the absolute freedom to choose, he, perhaps
unwittingly, opened the way for a truly liberating and noble
assessment of human personhood and wisdom. In his own
way, Moses was saying, "*Timshel*!" "Thou mayest!"

CHAPTER SIX

Between Promise and Fulfillment

"There's no hope, but I may be wrong!"
—A bumper sticker

"As a Christian, I am a prisoner of hope."
—Cornel West, The Other Side, 1998

Read Deuteronomy 31–34

Written over the gates of hell are the words, "Abandon hope, all you who enter here." Or so says Dante, the playwright of medieval fame. There are aspects of the Sinai desert that seem more like hell than anywhere else on earth. In mythology and reality, the desert is harsh terrain given over to earthquakes, snakes, scorpions, marauding bands of thieves, draught, burning sand, and desert demons to which Dante's description would aptly apply. After 430 years of living in Egypt, after the last plague sent the Egyptians begging for their departure, after the final swoosh of the Sea stopping their pursuers in their tracks, the fleeing Hebrew families must have thought they had truly arrived when they first hit the Sinai trail. Their revolutionary dance on the safe side of the Sea suggests they would not have believed it, even if Dante's sign would have been flashing in neon at the entrance to the Sinai: "Abandon hope, all you who enter here!" In their giddiness, emergent Israel, at first, danced and sang the song and dance of a free people. They acted like so many churchgoers who Annie Dillard, in her essay, "An Expedition to the Pole" calls, "cheerful, brainless tourists on a packaged tour of the Absolute." In their state of exhilaration, they may not even have been able to understand, if someone had warned them, that from the very moment of their departure (Exod. 12:41) until the end of the book of Deuteronomy, their grand hopes and dreams would die a thousand deaths, drowning in a sea of wilderness.

Little did they realize or could have known that their journey out of Egypt and into their promised future was a *via negativa*, a negative way to God. It would be a journey of leanness, of survival, of social dislocation, of exile—a journey of great price. So many of us who call ourselves Christian do seem like travelers on a journey of joy, happiness, and light, always ascending up, up, and away from darkness, loss, and chaos. James Lapp, in his essay, "Waiting in the Wilderness," suggests that most of us might even consider life's wilderness wanderings as okay "so long as we can vacation there." With our RHI backpacks and warm L. L. Bean hiking boots, we might even imagine making it for forty days and nights on the backside of a desert. But forty years?

Finally, on the Banks of Jordan

The congregation standing on the banks of the Jordan River listening to the final sermon of Moses had certainly learned by then that the harsh experience of passing through the Sinai was like passing through hell itself. The desert had nearly eaten them alive. The moment they left Egypt, they had complained about almost everything and who wouldn't have? Life seemed better in Egypt, even under slave conditions, than the torture of the desert. It seemed Moses was constantly battling, not only bandits from without, but demons from within. At one point, even Moses reached the point of complete exasperation and hopelessness. He could, perhaps, understand why God might abandon this unruly, ungrateful bunch of complainers, but how could God do this to him? He accused God of abuse and hurled questions into God's face (Num. 11:11-15): "Why have you treated me so badly? Why have I not found favor in your sight, that you lay the burden of all this people on me? Did I conceive all this people? Did I give birth to them, that you should say to me, 'Carry them in your bosom, as a nurse carries a sucking child,' to the land that you promised on oath to their ancestors? Where am I to get meat to give to all this people? . . . If this is the way you are going to treat me, put me to death at once!" These are good questions, to which we will return in a moment, questions that still remain after all these years.

But as for the people themselves, by the time they finally do reach the banks of the Jordan River, a whole generation of them had been killed either by venomous snakes bites, swallowed up by earthquakes, dead of thirst and hunger, bludgeoned in battle, or stoned in punishment. No wonder that among the first words of Moses to the survivors of the desert holocaust was an attempt at a rationale for why not one from that earlier "evil generation" would see the good land that God swore to their ancestors, except, of course, Joshua and Caleb. Only the "little ones," only those who had not yet reached puberty, only those of the next generation would make it (Deut. 1:35-39). Even Moses, himself, would end up dying in this hopeless hell-of-a-place.

The Unfair Ending

The biblical texts leading up to the book of Deuteronomy and the introductory sermon of Moses attempt to provide a *moral* explanation for why only a remnant survived the desert experience, though anyone who has ever been stuck trudging through the desert would need no more of an explanation than a natural one, namely, deserts devour people. Even if we are mostly persuaded by the moral explanations for why the older generation didn't make it, readers of the book of Deuteronomy might still be rightly puzzled on moral grounds for the treatment Moses gets in the end. Moses' earlier rage at God might still seem in need of explanation, moral or otherwise. "Tell us, God," we might legitimately ask, "in the name of all that's right and just, in the name of all that's fair, tell us, why? Why? Why doesn't Moses get to cross the finish line of a race well run? Of all people, why not, Moses?" The book of Deuteronomy says, "No prophet ever arose in Israel like Moses" (34:10). He met God "face to face" and lived. He was "unequaled" in "signs and wonders" (34:11), more humble than any other person on earth (Num. 12:3). Was Moses apparently good enough to lead the people out of Egypt (34:11), but not good enough to lead them into the Promised Land? And, for what? Moses died never getting to cross over Jordan's stormy banks. If anyone should've been able to cross over, it should have been Moses.

Twenty-six times in Deuteronomy and many, many more times before that, beginning way back in Abraham's day (Gen. 12), the LORD promises (on oath) to lead the people (Moses included) into a land flowing with milk and honey. In literary terms alone, even more so in reality, when it comes to Moses as the most likely of all people to receive the sworn promise of God, we the readers are set-up for disenchantment of the highest order. Those who have stood on Mt. Nebo in modern-day Jordan and gazed across the Dead Sea and the great rift of the Jordan Valley, have felt the anguish of dashed hopes and dreams that happened on this spot for Moses. I know I did. Our hearts break when we feel God's presence leaning over Moses' shoulder, pointing as it were, across this magnificent vista of his dreams and hear the LORD say to him (34:4b): "This is the land of which I swore to Abraham, Isaac and Jacob, saying, I will give it to your descendents; *I have let you see it with your own eyes, but you shall not cross over there.*" Whenever I read these words, the breath of hope is almost sucked from me completely. It feels cruel. It hurts. It's as if Moses is drop-kicked short of his life's goal. What utter disappointment! For Moses, Dante was right about his desert hell: "Abandon hope, you who enter here."

We have a hint of how much Moses wanted to enter the Promised Land way back in Deuteronomy 3:25. He pleads with God, "Let me cross over to see the good land beyond Jordan." The text itself seems at a loss for why Moses can't. Twice, Moses offers the blame-shifting attempt at explanation, suggesting it is the people's fault that he can't enter the land (1:39; 3:26): "The Lord was angry on *your* [Israel's] account, saying 'You also (Moses) shall not enter there!'" Apparently, for the editors of Deuteronomy, the first explanation seems patently unfair to Moses, as most readers would immediately react and say, "But that's not fair! Why should Moses suffer because the people were insolent?" So the editors, perhaps in an attempt to defend God a bit here, look for an additional explanation for why Moses doesn't get to receive the promise. They find an incident that might help to explain why Moses is, at least, partially responsible for the withdrawal of the promise. They remember back to an incident in which the people were once again complaining about needing water and Moses strikes the rock twice as he had done once before to get water. However, this time God had told him only to speak to the rock. The writers of Deuteronomy (32:51) suggest that it was this disobedient act by which both Moses and Aaron "broke faith with the Lord in the wilderness of Zin by the waters of Meribath-Kadesh by failing to maintain Yahweh's holiness among the Israelites." And as a result, neither will enter the Promised Land.

Even as a young child in Sunday school when I first heard the story of Moses striking the rock with his staff twice instead of just telling the rock to produce water, I wasn't satisfied that that little incident deserved the punishment Moses got. One could list the grievances God might have against Aaron, but Moses? My dad, who certainly wasn't God, would never have been so harsh for such an infraction. So why was God? A miracle worker's error in judgment, maybe, but, even then, the punishment seemed a bit over-the-top. Certainly, God didn't seem to be using the discipline of "logical consequence." Instead of a fifteen minute "time out," Moses was getting the ultimate time out, with no appeals. You shall not enter, period! "Never speak to me of this matter again!" rebukes Yahweh (Deut. 3:26) to a clearly disappointed Moses. Cruel and unusual punishment? I thought so in Sunday school and I still do. After all, it was the people moaning and complaining most of the time, not Moses. Moses was doing the best that any leader could be expected to do under the same circumstances. Flustered and frustrated, Moses taps the rock as he had done in the past, instead of merely speaking to it, and now he gets the ultimate heave-ho? It just didn't make sense to me. This is a case where the old saying about disappointment is true: Disappointment happens when just about the time we think we can make both ends meet, someone moves the ends. Given Moses' exemplary life of obedience, it seems God has moved the goal posts while the ball is in midair for the perfect field goal. Could it be that there is more than meets the eye, even in the narrator's feeble attempts at explanation, here? I think so.

At the beginning of this study, it was suggested that there's no reason and every reason the book of Deuteronomy is in the Bible. Keeping Moses out of the Promised Land seems an overreaction leading us to wonder, why bother with the book of Deuteronomy at all? The story in Numbers gives what it believes to be one reason Moses is kept out and as we suggested, we could read straight from the end of Numbers to the beginning of Joshua and not skip a beat in the story-line. Add to this the fact that the book of Deuteronomy ends without being able to adequately account for what even happened to Moses. Deuteronomy simply ends three great sermons later with the mysterious death of Moses saying simply (34:6): He died at God's command and "was buried" (by whom?) in a valley opposite the Promised Land, but "no one knows his burial place to this day."

Deuteronomy ends with its hero dead and the people weeping. There they stand by the willows weeping on Jordan's stormy banks casting "a wishful eye to Canaan's fair and happy land." Not much happiness here. It seems hope has been buried alongside Moses in his unknown sepulcher at the edge of a vast hopeless desert.

On the other hand, there is every reason the book of Deuteronomy is in the Bible. Perhaps the untimely death of Moses is not simply due to the seemingly unfair timing of God. There's more to it. Literally, and here literarily, the end of Moses sets the stage for a new beginning. At the end of Deuteronomy we see foreshadowed a more hopeful future (34:8): "The Israelites wept for Moses thirty days; *then* the period of mourning for Moses was ended."

If the meaning of a story is most often determined by the way it ends, what meaning should we infer from the fact that the book of Deuteronomy concludes with its hero dead and lost and his followers standing on the other side of Jordan looking across to the Promised Land? To make the point more emphatic, the end of the story of Deuteronomy also marks the end of the first part of the Hebrew canon, the Torah (the Pentateuch), Israel's first Bible. One would've imagined that a story so filled with promise of land (6:23; 26:9) would've ended with fulfillment, with a landed people. One would've thought that the earliest canon-makers would've included the book of Joshua in their first Scripture, telling as it does the great fulfillment having taken place. This is especially so since all the earliest oral creeds of ancient Israel all ended with Israel in the land and the promise fulfilled (Deut. 26:5-9). Why then, does the Torah, Israel's first Bible, end with Deuteronomy and not Joshua, which contains the fulfillment of the promise?

Once again, we see how the book of Deuteronomy is a crossroads book. It appears to have been inserted where it stands in the text between the books Numbers and Joshua as a literary crossover to help wandering refugees prepare to become a settled people, to pass from one generation to the next, to transform the old laws of Exodus to the updated laws described by its title, *Deutero-nomos*. It appears that the canon-makers used the book of Deuteronomy to get from the "there and then" of history to the "here and now" of liturgy. The book of Deuteronomy was not simply inserted to divulge more details so later historians could better understand what actually happened in the desert. As we have seen, it doesn't add all that much to the history of the events described that aren't already given elsewhere. The future remains open ended on the banks of the Jordan in this last book of Israel's first Scripture, even as we wait the fulfillment of the New Testament today.

On the Banks of the Tigris-Euphrates

We now know that the Bible in its final form began to emerge much later in Israel's history, when the people of God once again found themselves as refugees from the Promised Land standing by the waters of Babylon, picking their scabs on the ash heaps of history. Their great temple, their land, their kingdom, everything that had given them a sense of identity and destiny for some six hundred years since their desert wanderings, were all gone. Can you imagine what the Torah story sounded like to them, ending where it does with the book of Deuteronomy? A story that ends on the banks of the Jordan looking across to the promise of a homeland flowing with milk and honey had now become, truly, their story. The Jordan River might as well be the Tigris-Euphrates Rivers of Babylon. The hills of Moab overlooking the Promised Land might as well be the fertile crescent of Babylon where they found themselves now. The lessons outlined in the three sermons of Moses were the lessons they needed to hear again, as if they were among that new generation waiting for the promise to be fulfilled once again. The promise of "what still might be" was the promise they needed for themselves. The book of Deuteronomy held out hope. Hope. Sometimes that's all we have to keep us going. And sometimes that's enough.

Now for the refugees in Babylon, all the stories of the Torah became stories of hope, of promises made that still needed fulfillment, of decisions made that might be made differently. As was noted earlier in this study, the stories of

the Former Prophets (Joshua-2 Kings), following Moses laying
before the people the choice for life or judgment, now
became object lessons on how this new band of refugees
might do things differently, choose differently, if their own
future was to be different from that of their foreparents
whose decisions brought them into exile. Rabbi David
Hartman, an Orthodox rabbi and philosopher living in Israel
today, suggests how he reads the book of Joshua, "I'm here
to correct the mistakes of Joshua. I don't want to live with
Joshua as a permanent model of how Jews build the land."
So, the Bible, formed as it was in exile, became a means to
fully appreciate anew that their destinies were once again
wide open. They may do things differently this time around.
This time around, standing, as it were, once again on the
eastern banks of the Jordan River, they are given a second
chance to make different choices than those that eventually
drove them into exile.

Now the story of the first exile of Adam and Eve from the
Garden takes on new meaning. The story of Cain's exile to
the East of Eden, the story of God starting over after Noah,
and the story of humanity's grand architectural debacle in
Babel (Babylon!) are heard in fresh ways by people who are
on the brink of starting over again in their own exile. Indeed,
Abraham and Sarah, whose story begins in Babylon, but
who are called to a refugee life toward the Promised Land of
Canaan and their almost immediate exile to Egypt because of
famine would resonate with the people in seemingly permanent
exile in Babylon. In one of the central confessions of the
whole Torah, found in the book of Deuteronomy (26:5),
Abraham is described this way, "A wandering Aramean was
my ancestor and he journeyed down into Egypt!" He journeyed down into Egypt, down into slavery, down into
depression, down into undocumented "alien" status, down
into loneliness ("a few in number"), down into physical
abuse and torture (v. 6 "the Egyptians afflicted us and treated
us harshly); down into weeping, and wailing, and gnashing of
teeth (v. 7 "we cried out to the Lord"), down, down to Sheol,

down to the pit, down to the pole of absolute darkness, down into hopelessness. Abraham's grandson Jacob, soon to be named Israel, takes on new meaning in the story of his flight from Esau, who like Cain before him, sought to kill his brother. Jacob, with his new name Israel, flees into exile (to Haran in Babylon!) until finally he is, once again, able to return to the land of promise.

Living in Hope of Unfulfilled Promise

What is misleading about traditional readings of the Torah and subsequent readings of the desert wanderings and later exile is that the stories of the wanderings themselves and the stories of the later exile are hardly ever, if ever, read as theological innovations in their own right. We generally read them as straightforward accounts of history and often fail to appreciate their larger archetypal (literary) meaning for people mired in hopelessness. Often the focus of our readings are directed at the social and political restoration described in these stories, without fully appreciating their meaning as stories of the great failures of God's people. We have been so influenced by the ideologies of the Solomonic and later Constantinian state-apparatus, failing to see that, just maybe, to be people of faith like our spiritual foreparents Abraham and Sarah, God calls us to a life of wandering and standing on the banks of a stateless, boundary-less divide, living in hope of a yet fulfilled promise.

If we are people who pattern our lives after the people in the book of Deuteronomy, might there not be another biblical paradigm other than that of a people of the land, of state-hood, of temple worship, that more honestly presents the world as most of us know it and experience it more often than not? Might not the paradigm of our faith-existence be more like the religion of the landless people of the book of Deuteronomy, a wandering desert people, a people of faith living in a state of existential exile? Might our faith existence be more like a people whose identity rests not on the nation state, with all its power trappings, but on something far more enduring? A promised future? Edward Said, professor of comparative culture at Columbia University until his death in 2003, himself a Palestinian exile, describes such a people in his article, "The Mind of Winter: Reflections on Life in Exile." "The exile," he writes, "knows that in a secular and contingent world, homes are always provisional. Borders and barriers, which enclose us within the safety of familiar territory, can also become prisons and are often defended beyond reason or necessity. Exiles cross borders, break barriers of thought and experience." The book of Deuteronomy is a cross-borders book, inserted in the narrative of a wandering people, in order to break barriers of thought and experience.

Such a reading of the book of Deuteronomy would be good news to any native or aboriginal people whose lands have been annexed by the majority, to all people without countries to call their own, to all minorities without power, and all others who live in existential exile with little hope of political emancipation. From such a place of quasi-permanent exile, of diaspora peoples, where no Exodus experience has yet happened or has happened so many generations ago to be mostly irrelevant to their own experience, the story of God being present with them in the desert of their own experience may bring new hope of a future promise yet to be fulfilled.

And so, in reading the book of Deuteronomy, with its disappointing end, and yet-to-be realized future, ground is laid to understand so many of the stories of the Torah in a new way. Now we read these old stories in the same way as we might read the story of Christ's own journey down from Galilee to Jerusalem, down into Holy Week, down to the cross of exile. If the incarnation is anything at all, it is, in the words of Kathleen Norris, "the place where hope contends with fear." There are few places on earth more likely to evoke our deepest fear than the desert. And perhaps also, there is no greater place on earth than the desert to begin to understand the true meaning of hope. The ancient desert fathers, who sought to experience this primordial exile for themselves, called their wanderings in the desert the "dark night of the soul." It is the desert journey that all of us must make and most of us do in our lives of struggle. Sadly, all too often, we make that journey alone because the church just as often ignores this part of the journey or tries to package it in such a way to disguise the truth that narrow and tortuous is the way to God and few there are who find it. We forget that a whole generation was lost along the way to the Promised Land, as was Moses. These stories are our stories, the very ones the book of Deuteronomy pauses to explain through Moses, instructing every future generation never to forget. The way to the Promised Land most often goes through the *via negativa*, the negative way or experience, walking in the shadow of the valley of death.

Like Israel of old, we too are refugees of sorts, standing on the banks of our own Jordan Rivers, looking for a promised land, an abiding city, a place of rest, a home, salvation, shalom, or the coming again of Christ. We stand here weeping the loss of old familiar laws and ways of doing things, burying our most precious leaders or mentors or parents or therapists. We too are being asked to strike out on our own, to say good-bye to our known past for a life "away far over Jordan." Hoping for what might be possible. Then again, in our lifetimes, may not be.

Deuteronomy helps us hope for the possible, but also guides us when evidence or others shout down such hope as an impossibility. Moses didn't get all he hoped for—for reasons we don't fully understand. Deuteronomy invites us to hope not just for what's possible, that is standard to human endeavor—to hope is part of our human genetic code. Deuteronomy invites us to go beyond genetics, to go beyond the ordinary, to imagine something more, to fix hope to a promise. Hope then is no longer simply "a passion for the possible" as claimed by Kierkegaard, it becomes instead a "passion for the promise."

Saint Augustine suggested hope has two beautiful daughters. Their names are anger and courage. Anger at the way things are, and courage to see that they do not remain the way they are. Certainly Moses, sometimes angry and always courageous, models such hope for us. Vaclav Havel, the playwright President of the Czech Republic who spent many years in prison hoping against hope for a better future, was able to harness his anger and courage to continue to write underground plays and essays that became holy texts of solidarity and promise that eventually undermined the communist regime of his oppressors. He once said, when asked what hope was, "Hope is not the same as joy that things are going well, or the willingness to invest in enterprises that are obviously headed for early success, but rather, an ability to work for something because it is good."

A Witness of the Past and Hope for the Future

When all is said and done, the book of Deuteronomy, through its great spokesman, Moses, reminds us that no matter what, the Torah-story stays with us as a witness of the past and hope for the future. Even as Moses moves off the scene, the living word of Torah remains—now written down (31:9, 24) and sung (32:1-44) and goes with the people in and alongside the ark (10:1-5; 31:26) as a witness. If history is any indication, had Moses continued to live and had he made it across the Jordan River, in all likelihood, like so many founders of great religions before and since, he would have been made a god. The book of Deuteronomy set out to argue against any form of worship other than to the one and only God, so Moses was removed, in a sense because of his own message. As a result, and in his place, was left a story, a scroll. This was something portable, unlike land, temple, or monarchy, that could go with its readers anywhere and everywhere they might wander. The way the book of Deuteronomy ends—the way the Torah ends—is to open up the promises of God, to explain the intention of God, and to say what is necessary to realize those promises. But the Torah scroll does not guarantee land, security, and blessing. It is a word, mere words, which have become the Word of God for us.

In a sense, today God's word comes to us as a new law, a trito-*nomos*, a fourth, or a fifth *nomos* which finds its place alongside our Torah-Christ story. Dietrich Bonhoeffer imagined this when he wrote in his *Letters and Papers from Prison*: "It is not for us to foretell the day, but the day will come when people will be called to utter the word of God in such a way that the world is changed and renewed. There will be a new language, perhaps, quite unreligious, but liberating and saving, like the language of Jesus, so that people are horrified of it, and yet conquered by its power." This is the gospel of hope proclaimed in word. The book of Deuteronomy functions as a prophetic word with an open-ended future. It serves as the source-text for all futures imagined by the prophets in later Israel. In a sense, in form and content, the book of Deuteronomy is the Bible's first example of prophetic eschatology: the study of futures. Deuteronomy never stops calling us to remember, to listen, to obey, to choose rightly and, above all, to hope. Deuteronomy is a prophetic book inviting us to get ready to cross the Jordan. In a way, it leaves us there. We must take the next step and cross on over, hoping in the promise.

But even more than the scroll of Scripture that was formed as a byproduct of Israel's exile, another word of hope is introduced by Moses in his last will and testament. Moses uses the language of Christmas, Emmanuel language, God-with-us language. Moses promised us the presence of God in the desert of life. Jesus Christ would later reiterate what Moses had in essence already said years before. When Jesus himself is about to depart from his disciples after the resurrection, he comforted them with the words, "And remember, I am with you always, to the end of the age" (Matt. 28:20). Here in the book of Deuteronomy, Moses tells Joshua and the people that no matter what (31:8), "It is the LORD who goes before you and the LORD will be with you and will never fail you or forsake you. Do not be afraid; do not be discouraged." God will go before us, will not fail us, or forsake us as we walk into a tomorrow we can't control. Take courage!

God does not promise that all our hopes will come true. Certainly they didn't for Moses or his generation. Still, God promises to be with us whether they come true or not. Much later in the book of Revelation an illustration of such passionate hope is told at a time when the church's hope was severely tested by persecution. Denise Priestly, in her book *Bringing Forth Hope*, recounts the story of the pregnant woman in labor (Rev. 12). The panting, writhing mother-in-waiting is confronted by a great red dragon, perhaps Leviathan, lord of chaos, hovering over her waiting to devour the newborn the minute it's born. The story is an apt illustration of the new birth of the church about to be devoured by the Roman legions. It might also be an apt tale of Israel's own destruction and precarious rebirth so many times in the past. The mother of Revelation is certainly facing death and the loss of her long awaited baby. Against all hope, she appears still to hope in the promise for which her labor pains anticipated. She hopes in Emmanuel, God-with-her, no matter what. Looking the dragon, as it were, straight in the eyes, she gives birth. In essence, she brings forth hope in the face of horrible circumstances. In the instant of the birth of her new little baby son, he is miraculously escorted to be with God in the throne room of heaven. His mother flees to, of all places, the desert. There in the place where only fools might flee for protection, she finds an oasis prepared for her by God where she will be nourished indefinitely. So the end of the New Testament resonates with the book of Deuteronomy, the end of the Torah, where God's people find nourishment and protection against all odds. Hope is born in the desert.

"Hope Is All We Have"

Sometimes hope is all we may ever have. I have several dear Palestinian friends, who, even as I write, endure forms of harassment and humiliation unfamiliar to most of us today. One man my age, with thirteen children, told me of his two sons taken from his home while a gun was pointed at his head when he protested. They were tortured with electric shocks to their genitals and necks by Israeli soldiers only to be released ten days later without charge. Another friend told me she was ordered to take her clothes off in front of the soldiers who broke into her home, but refused. Still others tell of homes being shot up, round-the-clock curfews in 100 degree heat, and constant harassment and humiliation at check points in this Promised Land. The stories are unending. While staying in Tantur Biblical Institute on the Jerusalem-Bethlehem border, my friend Hytham, who came from the Occupied Territories to work as a gardner at the Institute each day, always greeted me with a wonderful smile and warm conversation. After all this, he always appeared hopeful. I asked him why he remains so hopeful without any signs of hope anywhere around him? He said, in part, it's because of his seventy-five-year-old father. His father, who has seen and experienced even worse things than he, wakes up every single morning hoping for a better day. Hytham has never given up because, like his father, he says, "hope is all we have." For Hytham, as for so many others like him, hope is believing in spite of the evidence until the evidence changes. I left Israel after a three month sabbatical humbled and more hopeful in spite of all evidence to the contrary because of people like Hytham and his father who have nothing but hope to live for.

Do we, in whatever our circumstance, believe Moses and Jesus when they announce to us that God's presence will never leave us nor forsake us, no matter what? Such a hope in the promise of God's presence is worth more than any other lesser promise fulfilled, whatever it may be. A former professor of mine, Rolf Knierim, was about to go into surgery for a brain tumor. Before going under anesthesia and the knife, he made a most remarkable comment: "I do not pray for anything, I simply pray to Yahweh." He needed no promised healing, no promised recovery, no promise of successful brain surgery. For him, Yahweh's presence was, simply, enough. God's presence is enough to get us across any Jordan River, however stormy its banks.

Hope may have been buried with Moses in an unknown sepulcher in the desert. It didn't stay there. Hope may have been buried in the sepulcher with Christ. It didn't stay there, either. Whether three days or thirty days, whether a moment or a lifetime, hope will rise again! In the Older Testament, and for the people of God gathered around Moses in the Sinai desert, hope arose as Torah—Scripture written. In the New Testament, and for all people of God gathered around Christ, hope continues to rise in new life. For all of us, hope stays alive in the Torah-Christ story because of books like Deuteronomy. The book of Deuteronomy is a constitution of hope, a crossroads book from there to here, from then to now, from this generation to the next, from utter despair to profound hope. Hope in God is investment in God's promise to be with us, no matter what. Hope in God frees us to cross the Jordan, to walk into any future that we might imagine but cannot control. God calls us to hope.

> *I am bound for the Promised Land,*
> *I am bound for the Promised Land,*
> *Oh, who will come and go with me?*
> *I am bound for the Promised Land.*

Chapter 1: On Jordan's Stormy Banks

1. Why do you wish to study the book of Deuteronomy? What do you hope to learn? Have you read this biblical book before? If so, what do you remember about it?

2. "On Jordan's story banks I stand," sings the old spiritual. Imagine standing on the banks of the Jordan River, or any river for that matter. What images come to mind? How might the words "and cast a wishful eye" apply to the people of God standing on the banks of Jordan? What do such words mean to you in your own life situation? What longings do these images conjure up for you?

3. Read Genesis 15:7-19; Joshua 24; Jeremiah 34:8-22. How are the various covenants described in these passages similar? How are they different from each other? What kinds of covenants (ceremonies?) do we participate in today? What are some similarities and differences between covenants today and those described in Scripture?

4. The young King Josiah, while renovating the temple, found what appears very likely to have been an old lost scroll of the book of Deuteronomy. He immediately institutes a series of reforms based on what he reads in the scroll he found. What are some of those reforms? Imagine what it might be like to find a long, lost and verifiably authentic "gospel" of Jesus. Imagine what the content of such a gospel might be. What are needed reforms in today's church that such a gospel might shock us into implementing?

5. As described in this chapter, how does the book of Deuteronomy lie at the crossroads between divine-human revelation? In what way might your words become the Word of God to others?

Chapter 2: Between Then and Now

1. Reflect on the meaning of William Faulkner's statement: "Memory believes before knowing remembers." How has this been realized in your own life?

2. In chapters 1–4, Moses recounted the events of Israel's past (slaves in Egypt, daring escape, wilderness wanderings, giving of the law) to a new generation.

•What importance was such remembering and retelling of past events to the new generation? What importance did such a review have for Moses?

•How might remembering the past (memory) help form your identity?

•If you could live twenty additional years in full health in every respect *except* for total memory loss, would you? Why or why not?

•How important are past memories for present and future meaning in life? If important, why? If not, why not?

•What stories from your past have helped to shape you into who you are today?

•How were these stories passed on to you? Are there older people in your life that can tell you about the past? What other sources are available to you for learning about your roots?

•What memories have already become part of the "standard story" of your life? Are there other events, experiences (good or bad), that are overlooked or ignored that could be included but usually aren't? Is it possible to tell your story differently? What are the costs and benefits of passing on your story while including certain parts and excluding others?

•What values or portions of your story (past and present) do you hope outlive you? How do you plan to pass on those values/traditions to those who follow after you? Are there younger people in your life that you can tell "your" story to?

3. In Deuteronomy, Moses updated for a new generation the older version of the Torah presented in the book of Exodus.

•How was his example of reading God's Word (revised and updated) followed in Christ's time?

•How might we follow Moses' example when reading/interpreting Scripture (Older and New Testaments) today?

Chapter 3: Between Grace and Law

1. If telling our stories (*muthos*; memory-sharing) plays an important part in forming our identities, how do biblical and other laws (*ethos*; ethics) contribute to making us who we are?

2. Moses and nearly all the prophets after him tried to call forth the spirit behind the law as motivation for following it (Deut. 5:6; 6:21).

•In your life, what has been (is) the best motivation for encouraging you to live by certain moral, societal, biblical values, norms or laws?

3. Certain laws in Scripture, as in life, become obsolete with the passing of time. Other laws in Scripture and life are expanded to include situations not originally intended or understood. Can you think of laws in Scripture, on our law books, perhaps in our nation's Constitution, or in life that may not have stood the test of time or have been amended or may need amending? On what grounds might you consider such amendation?

4. Obedience, by definition, implies obligation and setting boundaries. Moses equates obedience of God's Law(s) as choosing life. In biblical parlance this is called covenant-keeping. God is interested in creating and keeping relationships healthy and good.

•What positive obligations would you suggest are necessary (at minimum?) for making most relationships work?

•Is it humanly possible to live without or above the law?

•Describe a situation today in which obedience to laws could in fact be acts of grace, not simply legalistic requirements.

Chapter 4: Between Silence and God

1. Even before commanding the new generation to love God and each other, Moses commands them to "Listen!"

•Why do you think Moses insisted on such a posture *before* all others?

•How does the command by Moses to "listen!" mean more than just shutting up?

•Explain the proverb, "the one who opens her mouth, closes her eyes."

•How might you listen to/hear God speak today?

•How can (do) you create a listening posture in your life?

•How does complete silence effect you? Is such silence possible in your life? If so, how, when, where?

2. The *Shema* ("Hear, O Israel. . . ." Deut. 6:4-7) is Moses' positive version of the older first commandment that said, "You *shall have no* other gods before me. *Do not* make for yourself any idols. . . ." (Exod. 20; Deut. 5).

•Now, to the new generation, Moses emphasizes *loving* the one true God. Why do you suppose Moses revised the older more negative reading?

•Moses still seems concerned about God's unique status among alternative gods. Is such a concern still important for us to consider all these years later? If so, why? If not, why not? What other forms of gods do we manufacture and worship today?

3. The *Shema* calls not only for us to love God unreservedly, but also to love others whole-heartedly as well.

•Thomas Merton, the Christian monk, captures the essence of the *Shema* by saying: "Solitude and silence teach me to love others for what they are, not for what they say." What might he have meant by such a statement?

•How are listening and loving related to each other?

•How does listening and loving happen across generational boundaries? Between the sexes? Crossculturally?

Chapter 5: Between Life and Death

1. Moses laid before the new generation a clear choice with "logical consequences": either obey *all* the laws that he had just recounted (Deut. 5–28) and be blessed or disobey them and be cursed. He even included all future hearers (that's us) in his call to obedience (29:15). Yet, for us, some of the laws are outdated, and morally wrong.

•By what criteria do we decide that some of the laws of Moses should not be obeyed (risking by his definition, a curse) and which ones should be obeyed?

•What does our absolute freedom to disobey (or obey) even the best laws of Deuteronomy (or the Sermon on the Mount) say about who God is? Who we are? And how God wishes to relate to us?

2. The absolute freedom of conscience given us by God to choose to obey or not to obey stands behind a noble tradition of civil disobedience. Can you think of laws in this country that you might consider disobeying? If so, what are they? Under what conditions might you disobey?

3. Reflect on the apostle Paul's statement, "All things are lawful for me, but not all things are beneficial" (1 Cor. 6:12) or the statement by the Chinese housekeeper Lee in Steinbeck's novel, who said, "*Timshel*!" "Thou mayest!" What is the benefit (blessing) of such liberating statements? What might be the burden (curse) of such expressed freedom?

4. How might freedom of choice assist or detract from deciding how best to interpret conflicting, even contradictory biblical passages?

5. Can you think of specific important moral, ethical, theological, or personal decisions that you or others have had to make (past) or might face (now and future) that were made or still might be made using the Weslyan Quadrilateral (Scripture, traditions, experience, and reason) as a tool of discernment?

Chapter 6: Between Promise and Fulfillment

1. Imagine yourself as Moses, standing on the banks of the Jordan River looking across to the Promised Land, knowing he would never enter. Discuss the attempts by the book of Deuteronomy to explain his untimely death, his less-than-honorable burial, his exclusion from the Promised Land. Are the reasons given, adequate reasons? If so, why? If not, why not? In any case, what feelings might Moses have had?

2. Describe a time in which you have felt the disappointment, even despair, of opportunities missed or denied, of promises not fulfilled. How did you or do you cope in such situations? How did or do you view God as a result of such disappointment?

3. How are the lives of Jesus and Moses different or the same with respect to their teaching, their lives, their deaths, and the subsequent place of honor in the biblical accounts about them?

4. What spiritual benefit might be gained in passing through the *via negativa* (negative way) en route to an encounter with God or a deeper faith, even hope? What lessons might be drawn in comparing the book of Deuteronomy and the Christian experience of Lent and Easter?

5. How do you define "hope"? Can you give some examples of a hope-filled life in Scripture, in the lives of others around you, in your own life that may, on the surface, seem at odds with what may appear to be or feel like a hopeless existence?

6. How does the Negro spiritual, "On Jordan's Stormy Banks" (see quotes in the Introduction and at the end of this chapter 6), describe the book of Deuteronomy or incidents in history or in your own life? How do the words and melody of this song effect you personally?

7. What, if anything, have you learned in your reading and study of the book of Deuteronomy that is new, helpful, or challenging to your own faith pilgrimage?

Commentaries

Brueggemann, Walter. *Deuteronomy*. Abingdon Old Testament Commentaries. Nashville: Abingdon Press, 2001.

Miller, Patrick D. *Deuteronomy*. Interpretation Series. Louisville: Westminster John Knox Press, 1990.

Olson, Dennis T. *Deuteronomy and the Death of Moses: A Theological Reading*. Overtures to Biblical Theology. Minneapolis: Fortress Press, 1994.

Other

Brooks, Roger. *The Spirit of the Ten Commandments: Shattering the Myth of Rabbinic Legalism*. San Francisco: Harper & Row Publishers, 1990.

Freedman, David Noel. *The Nine Commandments: Uncovering a Hidden Pattern of Crime and Punishment in The Hebrew Bible*. New York: Doubleday, 2000.

Hillers, Delbert, R. *Covenant: The History of a Biblical Idea*. Baltimore: Johns Hopkins, 1969.

Kirsch, Jonathan. *Moses: A Life*. New York: Ballantine Books, 1998.

McKenzie, Steven L. *Covenant*. Understanding Biblical Themes. St. Louis: Chalice Press, 2000.

Sanders, James A. *Torah and Canon*. Philadelphia: Fortress Press, 1972; Reprint, Eugene, Ore.: Wipf and Stock Publishers, 2001.

Wildavsky, Aaron. *The Nursing Father: Moses as a Political Leader*. Alabama: University of Alabama Press, 1984.

THE AUTHOR

CAROL REWERS

James Brenneman is lead pastor of Pasadena Mennonite Church, a congregation he helped found in 1987. He teaches Hebrew Bible at the Episcopal Theological School at Claremont (Calif.). He is the author of *Canons in Conflict* (Oxford University Press), as well as numerous other articles in books, journals, and church publications. He teaches and lectures widely in universities, colleges, conferences, and churches. He lives in South Pasadena, California, with his wife Terri and their eight-year-old son, Quinn.